ACCLAIM FOR *S*

I enthusiastically endorse this book. It is not just a book, it is a journey into life. Through my experience in medicine, I have come to realize that there is more to life than contemporary science can explain, and that is the human soul. Ms. Ruth Rendely has proven this to be right. She has explained her life journey in a way that all of us can relate to, and, more importantly, through her knowledge and experience, she has given hope, belief, and love. I am truly impressed with her God-given talent, and her way to express it so that we all can understand and appreciate it.

—Adrian, Bocirnea, M.D.

"I'm thrilled to see that Ruth Rendely is helping people to make contact, and to work more intimately, with their companion angels. Nothing could be more important at this key point in the evolution of both species. When humanity moves, individual by individual, to fulfill its true destiny, it will be with our angels at our sides. This is an ancient promise and it is coming about in our lifetimes. May those with ears, hear."

—Timothy Wyllie, co-author *Ask Your Angels*

This book is a simple story of how one woman opened to the angels and then began to share what she learned with others. Slowly, as you read her tale, you will find shifts happening to you as well. Subtle is the technology of angels, not like knives or guns or bombs. It's a soft technology, and yet it's a powerful one.

—Andrew Ramer, co-author *Ask Your Angels* From the Foreword

Seraphim Blueprint *is a fascinating account of one woman's journey as she develops the power of healing by explicitly following the guidance of angels. Rendely provides a "must-read" book for anyone who believes in the power of angels to help guide us into becoming our best selves.*

—Randy Peyser, author *The Mind, Body, Spirit Speaker's Guide*

Seraphim Blueprint

The Power of Angel Healing

Ruth Rendely

Foreword by **Andrew Ramer**,
Co-Author of *Ask Your Angels*

To Pam —
Love to have you on
board.

Ruth Rendely

1ˢᵗ WORLD
PUBLISHING

Seraphim Blueprint

RUTH RENDELY

© Ruth Rendely 2007

Published by 1stWorld Publishing
1100 North 4th St. Fairfield, Iowa 52556
tel: 641-209-5000 • fax: 641-209-3001
web: www.1stworldpublishing.com

First Edition

LCCN: 2006940381
SoftCover ISBN: 978-1-4218-9907-7
HardCover ISBN: 978-1-4218-9908-4
eBook ISBN: 978-1-4218-9909-1

Please note that *Seraphim Blueprint* reflects the personal experience of the author and that of many of the individuals she has worked with. The book is not to be interpreted as an independent guide for self-healing. The information provided is intended to complement, not replace, the advice of your own physician or other health care professional, whom you should always consult about your individual needs and any symptoms that may require diagnosis or medical attention and before starting or stopping any medication or starting any course of treatment, exercise regimen, or diet.

In order to ensure the privacy of certain individuals mentioned in this book, names and places concerning those individuals have been changed.

Dedicated to:

My maternal grandfather
Abraham Popiel
Who taught me the power of silence

And his daughter
Juliet
Who molded my deep concern
For humanity

And to Princess Diana
For showing me that
One could be a great healer
And hardly know it

Acknowledgements

I thank Dzintra Ritenis for suggesting that I write this book, and Paula Kapp, one of my students, who graciously gave of her time to help with the early editing. I am grateful to Phyllis Butler for guiding me through the publishing maze. And I wish to thank my most appropriately-named dear friend Angela Mailander for being the perfect conceptual editor for this project, with an uncanny ability to merge with me in the process, along with sprinkling her deep spiritual wisdom like fairy dust here and there in the book.

I want to acknowledge also the people who really touched me deeply in this lifetime. I am eternally indebted to Maharishi Mahesh Yogi for sending me to spiritual "finishing school"; to Neville Rowe, the dolphin channeler, who early on recognized my gifts; and to the Reverend Joseph Martinez, the Filipino-American psychic surgeon, whose great intelligence and huge heart showed me how to be a hands-on spiritual teacher.

CONTENTS

Foreword

The morning news, the magazines we read, the conversations we have with family, friends, coworkers, even strangers on busses and standing in line, all remind us of this certain truth—that we as a species have made great progress—in advancing the technology of destruction. Wars rage across the planet, and storms rage, the result of our tampering with nature. The air is poisoned, the water is poisoned, and we have gouged deep holes into the surface of this once-perfect sphere. Its forests are vanishing, its wildlife is endangered, and yet we continue to perfect our killing ways.

Our morning newspapers, the sites we visit on the Internet, the reports our children write for their homework in school, all remind us of the deadly inventions of our culture. Many of us live in despair, feeling hopeless about the state of the world, feeling that there's nothing we can do to make a difference in the world. Some of us have taken up quiet spiritual practices, knowing that inner change is the path to outer transformation, but we may end up feeling that when we sit in meditation we're the Dutch boy standing with his finger in a hole of a leaky dike.

And yet there are alternatives, there are other ways to live in the world and make a difference. This book is one of them! The technology of killing is cold and hard. The technology of this book is soft, warm, radiant. It doesn't come to us from sterile laboratories, or from austere factories. It comes to us from the sweet, shared interaction of human beings and the angels. Yes, there was a time not too long ago when angels were a fad. Their faces appeared on wrapping paper and greeting cards. They smiled at us from the covers of books and calendars, promising us salvation. It's easy to dismiss angels, but please remember that our invisible friends have been known to every culture on the planet, in many different ways, with wings and without, with halos and without, always with a mission and always with a message—to help the human race in it evolution. And now, through the author of this work, they come to us, to you, in a different way.

This book is a simple story of how one woman opened to the angels and then began to share what she learned with others. Slowly, as you read her tale, you will find shifts happening to you as well. Subtle is the technology of angels, not like knives or guns or bombs. It's a soft technology, and yet it's a powerful one. And in an endangered world—what better story can we tell than one that offers not just hope, but techniques for making a difference in the world?

Reading this book will inspire you, and practicing the techniques that Ruth was given by her angel will empower you in the deepest and most heartfelt way, to remember that all of us have the power to make a difference in the world. As hopeless as things may seem, when we read about tsunamis and listen to reports from another war zone—it's not too late for us to make a shift in our journey and learn to live in the world in a new way. Share this book with those you love. Teach what you've learned to the people in your community. Spend time each day practicing what you learned here. Pour over the blueprints contained in this book just like the architect and builder that you are—of our new future, of our new world, shining and whole again, luminous and healed.

Andrew Ramer

San Francisco, California

Introduction

W hen Ruth asked me to do the final edit of this book, I happily agreed. After all, we'd been friends since the mid-seventies. We met because she was determined to have a gray kitten for her new flat when she moved to Iowa City to begin her doctoral studies at the University of Iowa. Somebody knew that my cat had just had a litter of kittens, and one of them was the exact color she was seeking. We hit it off immediately because we had a lot in common. We were both doctoral students—she in History, I in Comparative Studies, which is primarily a philosophy degree. We were also both involved with the Transcendental Meditation Program (TM), she as a teacher, I as a practitioner.

We remained friends ever since our years at the university; indeed, Ruth has been one of my closest friends. When I first met her, I had a keen interest in Jewish intellectual history, having translated a German-speaking Jewish poet for my M.F.A. in Translation Studies and was about to do extensive research on a Jewish writer, art critic, and philosopher who had been famous in Europe and the U.S. in the early 20th century, but who had been systematically forgotten during the Nazi era. Ruth, it seemed to me, was an embodiment of what was best in Jewish intellectual history. She had depth; she was brilliant, witty, charming, and her insight into others often seemed downright uncanny. Ruth did have a low tolerance, though, for nonsense, and people who were less serious and less honest than she is sometimes found her a bit critical. But in the context of graduate school, her analytical side was an asset. And I, at any rate, enjoyed her often hilarious, though sometimes acerbic, summing up of other peoples' foibles and weaknesses.

 It is easy to see all that in one of my favorite photos of her. Is it not obvious that the lovely girl in this picture could lay a man low with three or four well-chosen words? This photo is how I remember my friend from our student days. Since then, her sharp insight into others has deepened, and though she is still somewhat intolerant of nonsense, her critical side has mellowed into profound compassion.

As I was working with this book, there were two related things about Ruth that I thought didn't quite come through in her writing. The first and lesser of the two was that I wanted her to do a better job of explaining why she did not finish her Ph.D. at the University of Iowa. "I don't want people to get the idea that you couldn't cut it intellectually," I told her.

"Well," she countered, "Anything I say is likely to sound like sour grapes, and I truly no longer care. If I had gotten that degree, I'd be teaching history at some university now. And instead of a glorious adventure communing with an angel, I'd be attending boring faculty meetings and get a gold watch at my retirement."

I had to agree she had a point—two points, actually, one about sour grapes and one about gold watches. Still, I wanted to set the record straight. Ruth and I both had to deal with extreme prejudice because of our involvement with Transcendental Meditation. Ken Wilber, a practicing Buddhist, is probably the best-known New Age American philosopher, who has examined and documented the same prejudice Ruth and I faced, and he calls people like Ruth "courageous pioneers." Why courageous? Don't Americans enjoy academic freedom?

Because universities subscribe to philosophies, students and professors have academic freedom only as long as they remain within the confines of the philosophy and norms of their day. The philosophy of the seventies was deconstruction (deliberately using the lower-case spelling)—a philosophy that explicitly denied the existence of transcendental reality, "deconstructing" that reality as mere words—which the transcendent most definitely *is*, unless it is actually *experienced*. Obviously, adherents of deconstruction had not tasted the transcendent, and they have become famous for unrelenting arrogance and intolerance against those who had.

Back in the 70s, the prejudice against people like Ruth and me was particularly vehement at the University of Iowa for two reasons. First, the originator of deconstruction was the French philosopher Jacques Derrida, and one of his major champions and translators was, for a time, head of my department. Second, because Maharishi Mahesh Yogi established his university in Fairfield Iowa in 1975, just sixty miles south of the University of Iowa and because six percent of Iowa City's population had learned Transcendental Meditation while Ruth and I studied there, the deconstructors felt threatened with an "enemy" at the gates.

In my own case, after finishing the coursework and passing the doctoral exams, I knew that the academic establishment would accept nothing I felt like writing, even though I held my department's most prestigious fellowship. But though I did not submit a dissertation, I did write one, and later the most respected university press in my field accepted it for publication. If it had not been for that acceptance, I, too, might have felt, as Ruth did at the time, that I wasn't good enough.

I went on to start another Ph. D. in a related field and completed that one successfully. I do think that after finishing the coursework for two Ph.D.'s and passing doctoral exams twice, I am qualified to judge: there was nothing wrong with Ruth Rendely's dissertation. And the scientific research of the last thirty years has fully vindicated her thesis to the effect that the experience of the transcendent fosters creativity, as she demonstrated with the historical example of the Shakers.

That brings me to the second and more important thing I thought was not quite apparent in Ruth's writing, and that was the depth of her perception of others that I have already mentioned. In thinking about how best to give a reader insight into this aspect of Ruth, I decided that showing was better than telling. It is at my insistence, therefore, that Ruth has allowed the reprinting here of the following soul reading of Princess Diana, which she wrote right after Diana's death. We thank *The New Times* of Seattle for permitting its republication.

Angela Mailander

Diana's Spiritual Legacy

By Ruth Rendely (November, 1997)

Experiencing the collective mourning of Princess Diana in the week following her death, I groped to make sense of the great outpouring of grief. As a soul reader, I did a psychic reading on Diana for the first time and discovered that she was a walk-in. Her birth soul was a "wanderer," or "star seed," one that has spent many lifetimes on this planet but originally came from another star system to help raise the vibration of planet Earth. Between lifetimes, our souls explore other dimensions, and then we resonate with the highest compatible dimension in our next incarnation. Diana's birth-soul was vibrating in the tenth dimension, a level I call "guru-in-training." Tenth-dimensional souls are fairly common, especially in New Age circles. Thus, Diana's birth-soul would not have caused the sense of extreme loss that we were feeling.

Archangels foresaw the challenges Diana would face as Princess of Wales and wanted her to have a more spiritually accomplished soul. They coaxed the birth-soul out of her body, which provided an immense spiritual opportunity for the world.

When I examined the new soul, I was amazed. From the

Seraphim Blueprint

age of 18, Diana had a 14th dimensional Jupiterian soul, not literally from the planet Jupiter, but resonating to a Jupiterian archetype: vibrant, compassionate, radiant, joyous, and indestructible. The historical Buddha, Siddhartha Gautama, was of the same dimensional level. He was at an exceptionally high level for his time. His wanderings and ministrations were more private ones, while Diana's were in the public eye.

In my training as a meditation instructor, I had learned of the concept of *darshan*, a Sanskrit term that means the bestowal of powerful spiritual energies one experiences in the presence of a living master. It is a field-effect radiating out from the master 24 hours a day, every day, no matter what she or he is saying or doing. Such a field-effect also radiates from a photo of a master.

I saw that Diana was here to inspire. While initially it appeared that she had merely visited hospitals because it was her duty, in actuality she was a natural energy healer, unbeknownst even to herself.

As an energy healer, Diana felt a strong need to touch someone who was in pain and, like the advanced healer she was, she continually exchanged divine for human energy.

The more she used such energies, the more forcefully they flowed, ever brightening her energy field. Not only was she healing those she personally touched, she was also healing all those who looked at her photograph and gazed into her eyes. As American Natives well knew, the soul vibration is captured in a photo.

Diana didn't need, nor did she have any understanding of these mechanics. It is possible that the astrologers and psychics that she occasionally visited may have told her of some of these abilities, but it is likely that even they didn't know the nature of her gifts. Thus, she was unconscious of who she really was.

One might wonder why Diana wasn't aware of her own glorified status. I believe she thought of herself more in terms of her birth-soul image, "guru-in-training," and therefore felt the need to emulate a mentor like Mother Teresa. One can be spiritually evolved and still quite innocent!

Although these thoughts largely explain our collective grief, I still felt that an important aspect was missing. Under the first full moon following Diana's death, I began free-associating about her death and received a flood of strong impressions. Tuning in to the collective unconscious, I realized that Diana's death was triggering the infinite loss we all feel over the suffering and fragility of human life.

I personally was comparing her life and death to those of Christ. There were just enough symbolic similarities to trigger this comparison. Both died in their thirties. Both were hounded figures just before their death, and both were denied by their respective royal rulers. Both experienced human sorrow and felt doubt; both in a sense expiated our sins.

Since I can access soul information regardless of whether the soul is wearing a body or not, when I heard of her death, I investigated her whereabouts. Her soul was spending most of its time with her sons and her brother. She will continue to spend the next 11 months in the company of loved ones before leaving the earth plane to refresh herself. It is likely that she will reincarnate in approximately seven years in Australia.

The absence of the unique expression of her archetype in a physical body empowers that archetype to elevate us all, whatever that means to each of us—volunteering at a hospital, expressing our own gifts, or dignifying all we do with the embodiments of her grace. She inspired us to embrace the best of who she was.

PART I

THE SOURCE'S APPRENTICE

The Early Years

Why is the white stone still dancing in my hands? The English School closed down five years ago. Why haven't the energies they put into the stone ceased! No one to ask. The couple that ran the School split up. I've never met them, and it's nearly impossible to find them now.

All I have is a small stone that emits signals only I feel. Sometimes I test this by giving it to friends to hold, but they feel nothing. Yet in the early days I wasn't able to hold the small polished, egg-shaped stone for more than a few seconds before it became too hot. Now I can handle it for about an hour or more.

It's irreplaceable. In some strange way it evokes past and future knowledge. I travel with it tucked into my purse, away from curious eyes. When facing a crisis, I hold it tightly in my right palm, unbeknownst to anyone. Every time it's done the trick; I'm in command.

Years before the stone came into my hands; there were several important influences on my spiritual apprenticeship, including first and foremost a strong conviction that there is no God. This may seem strange to mention as part of a spiritual apprenticeship, but in thinking back, I realize it allowed me to be open to the reality of experience, which is often obscured by belief systems consisting only of words. Too often I've seen people who worship their religion instead of worshipping the Creator. Now I thank Him for humoring me, because although I grew up in an observant, orthodox Jewish household in Brooklyn, New York, I doubted God's existence as soon as I was told about Him. To please my mother, though, I went along with the whole God pretend-thing for a while by muttering my bedtime prayers. But soon after I stopped playing with dolls, around the age of three, I also stopped pretending to pray to an imaginary "God."

Unlike some children, I never saw angels, fairies, or make-believe friends. I had no memorable psychic experiences growing up and am unaware of such experiences in any of my ancestors, although my aunt Pauline was good at picking horses. I was a good child, bookish and serious. I loved school and, later, spent much of my adult life reading, study-ing and teaching.

When my younger sister Marsha and I were in our twen-ties, something occurred that changed our lives. Marsha was, and still is, the all-American beauty with luscious chestnut-red hair and skin so fair that our doctor advised my mother that she needed to stay indoors, out of the sun. Nor was her sensitivity limited to her skin; in her early twenties, while she was away at graduate school, she became seriously depressed. At the time I was her only confidante, but I was preparing to leave for a yearlong stay in Japan. We were living thousands of miles apart, so before I left the country I called her constantly, hoping she would stabilize.

Eventually, after learning to meditate and practicing con-scientiously, she started to heal. I was skeptical, however, about any meditation movement that involved a guru. Yet, I saw that the practice was good for her fragile psychological state, and she steadily improved.

At that time—the early seventies—I regarded meditation movements as faddish fringe phenomena. When my parents learned the practice, however, I realized I was the only one in the family who wasn't meditating. By then, I was a stressed-out, new high school teacher living in Honolulu. And so the next time my sister mentioned it, I agreed to learn, simply to calm me down, but I was determined not to allow myself to be brainwashed by any guru. Coincidentally, the Transcendental Meditation (T. M.) Center was about three blocks from my home in Honolulu.

After a year of meditating, I recognized that my stress levels were dropping—despite my increasing dissatisfaction with my teaching job. In a case of sibling reversal, I turned to Marsha for guidance in setting a new life course. She suggested that if I needed a new direction, I might want to take her job as Director of Admissions at Maharishi International University in Santa Barbara, California, since she was planning to attend a short Transcendental Meditation teachers' course in Europe with Maharishi Mahesh Yogi. By that time, late 1973, I was living and working in northern California, so it was easy for me to move to Santa Barbara in southern California.

The position paid room, board, and a $75-a-month stipend. The main reason others were interested in working for these slave wages was to earn course credits toward becoming a meditation instructor. At the time I felt such a course was an opportunity for me to 'get my head together' and plan my next 'real' life situation. If I worked long enough in Santa Barbara, I would earn the half-year meditation teacher-training course to be held at a Swiss resort. At the very least, this promised to be a great vacation.

With each passing week at the Santa Barbara meditation university, my skepticism was challenged as I saw new students mellowing within bare weeks of arrival at the school. When I had been working there six months, events transpired in such a way that I was able to go to Europe to attend the first three months of teacher training in the Italian Alps.

Young male Transcendental Meditation instructors conducted the courses for Maharishi in those years because Maharishi rarely put in an appearance. Although I had greatly enjoyed meditation for a year and a half, I still doubted many lessons in the course, including Maharishi's alleged sainthood. Photos of him showed a middle-aged Indian man dressed in orange robes with soft eyes, a moustache, a beard and long black, unkempt hair. I couldn't decide if he looked like a saint or a charlatan. When, he actually showed up for our small course in Livigno, Italy, however, something unexpected happened.

In preparation for his possible visit, I had been formulating a few challenging questions to ask him concerning women's liberation. I knew from listening to his audiotapes that the Western concept of women's liberation was diametrically opposed to his cultural background and thinking that was steeped in the ancient Vedic texts. I planned to corner him with these questions, but to do so with the sweetest tone in my voice to let him know that even a semi-enlightened soul was still concerned about women's rights. Maharishi arrived on July 23rd, 1974 and met with us late that evening. I was too nervous to pose any questions during that first session. By the following day, though, I had found the courage to go to the microphone. I had carefully rehearsed my first question.

"Maharishi, in many of your recorded tapes motherhood is glorified in the highest terms. But in this non-dharmic, or adharmic age (of Kali Yuga)[1] motherhood is either postponed or not available to many of us. Do the Vedas bind women to certain roles or activities? Or, as meditating women aspiring to higher states of consciousness, are we supposed to follow these roles even though the times are not suitable?"

Upon hearing my question, he turned toward me with a broad smile and in his thick Indian accent said: "Go get a chair and sit by the microphone." During previous sessions nobody had been asked to sit by the mike, so I was confused by his request. But other students whispered to me that I would be there for a while.

His thirty-minute answer was extremely diplomatic. In his distinctive style, he spoke carefully, building his case. I strained to stay focused and take in the meaning of what he was saying. First he established the authority of the ancient Indian texts known as the Vedas:

"The Vedas prescribe the mechanics of creation. Within the range of the Vedas lie all means of creation. It's impossible for a man not to act according to the Vedas, because knowledge is at the basis of action. The word 'Veda' just means knowledge. Veda, therefore, is at the basis of creation.

"Any culture's values are dependent upon climate and geography," he said, "And all progress is based upon the cultural values of the land. A civilization will thrive and evolve

[1] Ancient Indian culture assumes that the world passes through a continuous cycle of these four ages: Satya, Treta, Dwapara and Kali. Kali, the last age, is mercifully much shorter than each of the other three and it is an "adharmic" age. "Adharma" is the Sanskrit term meaning not aligned with one's life purpose, while the word "dharma" means aligned with one's life purpose.

as long as it is in accordance with the laws of nature particular to that part of the world."

He went on to say that when foreign influences are introduced to a culture, the compatible elements would be adapted and integrated into the host culture, while incompatible elements would be rejected. He made clear that it was a case of proportions. If foreign elements were introduced too quickly, or in quantities too large, the host culture might be damaged, but in small doses the new elements could be more readily absorbed, and be beneficial to the host culture.

For our role as future T.M. teachers, he said: "Meditation makes every culture a fertilizer for every other culture . . . . . Our role in the world is in preserving and enriching every culture with all its differences."

> A civilization will thrive and evolve as long as it is in accordance with the laws of nature particular to that part of the world.

Though he had skillfully skirted my question, this part of his answer nevertheless made me breathe a sigh of relief, as it indicated his willingness to compromise regarding the introduction of Indian cultural values into American society.

He finished by saying: "Every nation will be strong. Individualism in every nation will be strong. Men in every nation will have a strong manly identity. Women will be strong in their womanly positions. This will strengthen motherhood and fatherhood with no threat to any. We don't mind what the situation has been. We know it will be better."

At the time, his fresh perspective overwhelmed me. Over the years as I have watched various nations struggle with the introduction of foreigners or foreign influences, I often think back to Maharishi's organic answer, and the image that readily comes to my mind is of someone experiencing indigestion from trying to eat too much foreign food too quickly. I had come to think of different cultures as whole and individual beings, each with a distinct personality.

By the end of my turn at the mike, I felt a huge energy shift within my body. The combination of Maharishi's powerful *darshan* (enlightening energies) with the charm of a master teacher was too much for me. A few minutes earlier I had been a skeptic, but now I found myself becoming a devotee—plucked like a piece of ripe fruit.

In the days and weeks that followed on the course, I felt myself filled with childhood wonder—open to all sorts of new experiences. I sometimes found myself walking outside and noticing that the leaves on the trees sparkled, as if I had never seen leaves before, each one a witness to its own profound and intelligent life, yet connected to mine with beauty and meaning. Many people have had drug hallucinations like this, but I was not on drugs, nor had I taken any previously that could have caused flashbacks. Blake once said, "When the doors of perception are cleansed, man will see things as they truly are, infinite."

One day, after I had returned from the course, I was rereading *The Analects of Confucius*, a book I had studied for my master's degree in East Asian history, when suddenly certain phrases stood out in bold type. The text was not actually written that way, but as I turned the pages some unseen force seemed to be putting certain phrases into a bold format. Words we read ordinarily seem fleeting like ghosts, mere shadows of the realities of which they speak. Again I

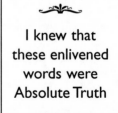

I knew that these enlivened words were Absolute Truth

thought of Blake, each word, each thought expressed in words filled immensities of meaning in heart and mind, and I knew that these enlivened words were Absolute Truth.

That afternoon as I read, I felt I had been given the keys to the universe. This feeling of awakening was sufficient to shake off as untenable any notions of atheism or agnosticism. I began to accept that we are spiritual beings and that God is. For the first time in my life I felt truly alive and optimistic. I was thirty-one years old.

What Maharishi didn't tell us exactly was that there would be a price to pay for this awakening. He did talk about the release of stress from our bodies, but he didn't say that this could mean the well-known "dark night of the soul" that almost all mystics talk about. When I consider that this dark night is typically eighteen to twenty years in duration, I feel lucky. Looking back now, I think somehow we can shorten this nightmare for future generations. A dark night of the soul lasting twenty years is just too much waste of human life.

The Pivotal Years

As the result of a cost-cutting measure, I lost my job at the T. M. university without much notice. But I didn't really mind since I figured that I had spent enough time cocooned in the T. M. Movement and needed to live in the real world for a change. I began formulating a new plan based upon my newfound mental powers. It occurred to me that now I could possibly tackle a doctorate in my favorite subject of history.

That had seemed too daunting for me earlier, but I realize in retrospect that the real reason that I had found it "daunting" had a lot to do with my being part of a generation of women who were fearful of becoming too smart for the men in their lives: I felt that a doctorate would end my rather feeble social life.

Since I had always managed to get full scholarships for my previous studies, I promised myself that I would do the advanced degree only if it were financially easy. I made a big mistake, though; I only applied to the University of Iowa, which was sixty miles from the new home of Maharishi International University. Again, the mistake was based on fear. I was afraid of being at any distance from the T. M.

Movement's *darshan*, and also I felt that, having interrupted my education, it was unlikely that any university would give me a scholarship at age thirty-three.

But, lo and behold, the University of Iowa's Department of History gave me a full scholarship for doctoral studies. They also gave me a plum job as a teaching assistant, with a subsistence salary.

At the time, my new departmental advisor, Prof. Stow Persons, was the national doyen of American intellectual history. I worshipped the ground he walked on, but when he warned me that he was likely to retire in less than two years, and that other people in the department might not be suitable to help me finish the degree, I brushed aside his comments. I really had no idea that a dissertation director pretty much had the power to decide whether I got the degree or not.

I had four fabulous years doing class work and in my spare time managed to change Iowa State Law by starting a non-smokers' rights group at the U. of I., to reflect the non-smoking movement that was just beginning to take hold in the U. S. When I passed my doctoral exams, Prof. Persons made a big point of thanking me for changing the University's rules so that faculty meetings were no longer smoky.

Although Stow Persons did not quit as soon as he had said he would, he nevertheless did resign when I was only six months into writing my dissertation. Little did I know how hostile most of the History Department was to the fledgling little university sixty miles south of their domain. Maharishi International University had a few years earlier bought a bankrupt college in Fairfield, Iowa. Its arrival on Iowa's academic scene was especially irritating to those living in the Bible Belt of America, whether they were academics or not.

After the Jonestown disaster in 1978, in which 900 people committed suicide at the orders of their cult leader Jim Jones, T. M. got brushed with cult tar, and I didn't know that the dissertation adviser, whom I had picked to be Person's successor, really had it in for the T. M. Movement. I was soon to find out, though, when he commented on my first draft on "The Foundation of Ecstasy: The American Shaker Experience, 1800-1850."

For the next five years he regularly rejected drafts of my dissertation, to the point where it actually got weaker as a result. One of his biggest complaints was that no matter how hard I tried, I couldn't find evidence *against* my thesis that Shaker inventiveness and creativity was evidently directly due to their ecstatic experiences.

Meanwhile, not only was the intellectual climate at the University of Iowa becoming tedious to me, I had also grown tired of the social isolation of being in Iowa, and longed to return to a more vibrant cosmopolitan community.

I moved to Cambridge, Massachusetts in 1980 and took a part-time job on staff at Harvard. I worked on my thesis with lessening enthusiasm as time passed. My final year at Harvard was my best position there—I was the program coordinator for the Program on U. S.-Japan Relations. It was really a high-profile program, with famous international politicians and diplomats often attending our small group conferences. It whetted my appetite for all things Japanese, and I returned to Japan in 1985, intending to stay in Tokyo for the next few years.

Having successfully relocated, by the fall of 1986 I was in a whirlwind head-over-heels-in-love romance with a tall, dashing, wealthy Japanese businessman, who seemed extremely devoted to me. I thought Takehashi was perfect for me. I was weak, however, due to chronic bleeding from uterine fibroids that I wouldn't let the Japanese doctors operate on. Takehashi was there every evening to be with me, as I endured severe anemia and looked anorexic. He was so completely attentive, that I thought we might even marry. Although as a rule, Japanese men will not marry foreigners, considering he had divorced a Japanese woman, I thought he might be willing to break from the usual taboo and marry me. I had a slight intuition though, that maybe he was not being fully genuine, but I ignored it. Though easier said than done, not ignoring slight intuitions was the lesson I learned from him.

When we were six months into our relationship, and I was told that my mother had less than a month to live, I began to feel him pulling away. I got the call from my sister in late November that my mother was dying of melanoma, that the skin lesions that had been operated on four years earlier, which she had told us were benign, were actually malignant, but she had not wanted to scare us. My life might have been considerably changed had my mother been initially truthful, because I wouldn't have lived ten thousand miles away from her for an open-ended stay. I could not believe that my beloved mother could actually be dying at 74, when I thought of her as healthy and destined to live a long life. My father, on the other hand, who had smoked unfiltered Camels most of his life, and who, after being hospitalized with full-blown tuberculosis, continued smoking two packs a day for 20 years after that, survived until he was 88.

During the Christmas/New Year's break, I returned to Florida to be with my mother and to relieve my sister, who had been with her until that time. While everybody else was celebrating the holidays, I was immersed in running my parents' household because the hospital had finished the chemotherapy, had given my mother two weeks to live, and had put her in our care at home.

Believing strongly in alternative methods of healing at the time, and trying to save her, I had put four psychic healers on my mother's case. Two were in Japan and two were in America. One of them was a female Hawaiian Kahuna, living in California, who seemed to me the most in tune with spirit—she did whatever they do, yet to no avail.

A week before my mother died, I suddenly thought to give her a full-body massage. The Kahuna suggested that I use olive oil scented with fresh rosemary leaves. I found the leaves and did exactly as told. My mother said that the experience was "heavenly." On January 1st, 1987 before celebrating the New Year with my family, I gave her another full-body massage. That day, when my sister came back after a three-week absence and greeted our mother, mother asked me "Who is that man who just entered the room?" Maybe because of her short hair, my mother thought my sister was a man. I replied, "Mother that is not a man! That is your daughter Marsha." Mother then said, "T. M.," probably in reference to my sister having influenced the whole family to meditate. Those were her last words. Sometime during our dinner in the next room, she expired.

On the plane back to Tokyo two weeks later, I was so scared of flying that I kept saying to my mother's spirit that I wasn't ready to join her yet, so that the plane wouldn't crash. I was surprised when Takehashi didn't meet me at the airport, but he confessed the very next day that during the last three months of our relationship he had been dating another woman, and that he planned to marry her.

My beloved mother was dead, the man of my dreams had

left me for another woman, and my intellectual and career aspirations had come to nothing. My memories of the first half of that year are a disheartening blur. I realized I was deeply depressed, and even wondered why I was not suicidal. Given my recent experiences, I was expecting suicidal thoughts to flood in at any moment. I did have the presence of mind to seek counseling and first went to a Protestant minister even though I was Jewish. Somehow, I didn't want people who really knew who I was to know about my severe depression. Going to a minister for counseling gave me some anonymity.

When that didn't work, I finally decided to seek religious counseling from someone of my own faith. I made an appointment with the only rabbi in Tokyo, a fellow New Yorker, a loquacious, slender man about ten years my junior. Ignoring his youth, I expected a certain amount of wisdom and gravity to be intrinsic to his station.

After listening to my ten-minute monologue on all my woes, the rabbi merely said, "And you *still* have a job and a roof over your head?" His practical, one-sentence answer, without a hint of pity, caused me to burst out laughing. This was the best medicine for what ailed me. It was April, and the first time I had laughed that year.

It was only a momentary reprieve, however. I was more than just depressed, it seemed to me. I was suffering so profoundly I could hardly breathe. I tried to reason with myself: Other people lost their mothers, other people lost their boyfriends or even their husbands, and other people's dissertations were not accepted. But this tactic did not help.

Then I tried to justify my suffering on the basis that my relationship with my mother had been unusually close. A few centuries before Freud wrote about parental attachments, the

Tibetan Book of the Dead noted that people generally have a difficult time with whichever parent shares the same sex with them, but in my case, that did not apply—not only did I love my mother almost as much as life itself, she seemed a perfect mother to me. The same thing applied to Takehashi: I couldn't imagine a man more devoted and attentive to my every need, at a time when I was very needy. And the failure of my attempts to write a doctoral dissertation that was acceptable seemed to call into question my most treasured trait at that point in my life—my intelligence. My mother, my boyfriend, and my attempts to get a doctorate seemed to be who I was, my core being—and who I was had died with my mother.

Of course, the rabbi was right: I had what I needed to live: a job and a roof over my head. And yet, as I said, the very foundations of my existence had disintegrated. All that I was and all that I had valued was not only gone for now, it was gone forever. This was something the rabbi did not seem to understand, or did not choose to understand, maybe for my own well-being.

There are still too many counselors who do not understand the differences between a situational depression, a clinical depression, and what has been called "the dark night of the soul," purported to be a precursor to enlightenment. They are three different things, and they need to be recognized and handled differently by anyone who is trying to help a person through a difficult time.

In a situational depression, people can be given hope and, when appropriate, can be counseled to change the situation. In a clinical depression, people can be helped with counseling and with medicinal herbs, or the intervention of a psychic healer. But in the dark night of the soul, the truth of the matter is that the small, individual self is dying, as it must if there is to be spiritual growth.

True, there were seemingly external causes, as there always are, but it is important to understand that they were not really causes so much as they were a "hook" for me to hang things on. Inspiration needs a local name and habitation. So, it seems, does the depression of the dark night of the soul. And I wonder if the caterpillar, who must literally dissolve into liquid inside of his cocoon before he can restructure himself as a butterfly, also feels the agonies of the dark night in which all he knew dissolves.

Two Mentors: One With a Body, One Without

Hoping to help my recovery from depression, I was thumbing through an old copy of *The Autobiography of a Yogi* by Paramahansa Yogananda in early May of 1987. This book had become a bible to many Transcendental Meditation teachers, as Maharishi often spoke about the special quality of living in an ashram with his master, but he had never actually written about his experiences. When Maharishi told us that Yogananda's book came closest to describing his own youthful devotional experience of living with his guru, many of us read Yogananda's *Autobiography* in order to understand Maharishi better.

In my first reading of this book several years earlier, every word had rung true even though the adventures described were so extraordinary and miraculous that one could hardly imagine experiencing them in a human body. Yogananda spoke about living swamis who were seen in two places at once, saints that levitated, and even one saint that never slept. In each case Yogananda witnessed these phenomena and wrote about them so compellingly that I came to believe that humans were capable of doing what most people consider to be science fiction.

Yogananda's spiritual lineage traced back to a semi-mythical saint called Babaji, a name that translates simply as 'revered father.' The book stated that Babaji was an avatar— an incarnation of the divine in a human body. The birth and origins of Babaji were unknown, but it was thought that he was hundreds and possibly thousands of years old. Over this long span of time his body stayed ever youthful with the handsome visage of an androgynous twenty-five year-old.

So that morning in May of 1987, following my usual meditation, I picked up Yogananda's book and opened to a discussion of Babaji which included the following: "Whenever anyone utters with reverence the name of Babaji, that devotee attracts an instant spiritual blessing." I thought why not try to connect with him? Rather than calling him out loud, I tried calling him mentally. Within twenty seconds, a powerful flood of energy entered my body, and light filled my head. I could feel the warm presence of his love and a sweet melting in my heart.

Whenever anyone utters with reverence the name of Babaji, that devotee attracts an instant spiritual blessing.

I was incredulous! This was the avatar described over and over again in the book as being extremely elusive. I believe Yogananda himself only saw him on one or two occasions in his whole life, and Yogananda was a highly enlightened soul. I failed to comprehend Babaji's presence in my bedroom.

I cried out: "Thank you, Babaji. Thank you!"

Because I was unable to see him, I kept switching back and forth between thanking him and doubting his presence. Still his energy kept pouring into my body.

Seraphim Blueprint

Now, Babaji tells me that he was relieved that I had finally made a conscious connection with him, although tenuous at best. It was as if I had put some kindling on a small pile of wood and had lit it with a match, while he was fanning the flames. He was waiting for the fires of my spirituality to take hold, so I could be an instrument for his work. At that time, I didn't know how long he had been waiting, or that he had been waiting at all. For me, in this lifetime, it was all new and unbelievable.

I should probably explain that, unlike some psychic spiritual seekers, I don't see the beings I'm in contact with. I feel them. Their presence has to be indicated through one of the six senses and, in my case, it's what I assume to be the finest sense of touch.[2] I feel their presence. You might say it's a kind of "psychic tingling." Albert Einstein once wrote about his own amazing thought processes "The words of the language, as they are written or spoken do not seem to play any role in my mechanism of thought." Instead, he wrote that his thinking was a "combinatory play of psychic entities." That " combinatory play of psychic entities," then has to be communicated somehow, in Einstein's case—through mathematical symbols, in Mozart's case—though musical notes, and in my case—through thoughts in my mind. This is about as close I as can get to describe my psychic/spiritual abilities, as Western languages are not really suited to speaking about spiritual phenomena.

This spiritual meeting with Babaji signaled a huge change in my life, which, over the years, has resulted in a whole new theory about souls, a theory I am still in the process of exploring.

[2] At their deepest level all senses are one, which is why poets so often use synesthesia: images in which hearing a sound is described (and experienced) in terms of seeing a color.

Maharishi had strict rules for all the teachers who were part of the T. M. movement. We were not supposed to be involved with any other spiritual teachers or practices. Seeing beyond this restriction, I broke out of this mold and allowed Babaji to guide me through what would be my second spiritual awakening. He was waiting in the wings, preparing me on more subtle levels for some new adventures and readying me for my meeting with Stewart, the Tokyo representative of the "English School," the following August.

I met Stewart through another part of my effort to find relief from my dreadful internal turmoil, and with the help of the slowly building guidance that seemed to be emanating from within me, from which source I knew not at the time. Over that summer, my experience of Babaji's energies slowly faded, and I just assumed that my experience of him that May was a singular event. I was wrong, but I didn't know that for several more years.

In order to kick off my social life and bring me out of my doldrums, I started a social club, since I had wanted to have a salon in my house for as long as I can remember. I called it the "Tokyo Leisure Club," TLC for short, and took some pleasure from the thought that this club would be "Tender Loving Care" for me. So I placed an ad in a Tokyo English language magazine mentioning that our club met twice a month. In anticipation of its success, I arranged for a series of interesting speakers. Since everything regarding the formation of this club went so smoothly, I assumed that I was taking the right steps to bring back some normality into my life. I had previously been a fix-it sort of person, and in this case I was observing an Amish proverb, "If you pray for potatoes, have hoe in hand."

Stewart called one day, seemingly out of the blue, but of course, he'd seen my ad. He was a Jewish-American, alpha male who took complete charge of every conversation with intelligence, finesse, and humor. I identified with him immediately. Our first conversation lasted about an hour, and I found myself trusting him more than seemed reasonable for a first meeting over the phone. My inner excitement about all that he suggested told me that I was on track, because becoming really excited about an opportunity is often a sign that your highest guidance is enthusiastic about the step you are about to take.

I learned later that Stewart had been part of the Muktananda training, and knew healing modalities from many cultures. Officially, though, Stewart was a Rolfer. Ida Rolf (1896-1979) was an American medical scientist who invented a form of deep-tissue muscle massage to release emotional blockages that helped straighten the spine. She trained legions of practitioners in this extremely painful technique in which the Rolfer twists your limbs as if wringing clothes dry. Fortunately, her most recent followers have found less painful ways to accomplish what she had set out to do, since it is true that emotional blockages can lodge deeply in muscle tissue.

There are, however, other subtle, profound ways to release such blockages. Maharishi would sometimes say that there are two ways of becoming enlightened, either via the body, or via the mind, because they are really two sides of the same coin. He put yogic practices on the side of the body, and he put meditation on the side of the mind. Given his mission, he led us to believe that the mind was more powerful than the body in becoming enlightened.

Stewart, however, recommended Rolfing for everything that ailed me, but when I said I was not interested, he seemed determined to sell me *something* and said: "I have just the thing for you—a healing crystal."

The word crystal instantly made me think of Atlantis, even though I was only vaguely aware of that 'lost' continent. Without hesitating I said, "I want one. But how does it work?"

"It's programmed with thought."

"What do you mean?"

He was cryptic in his reply, but I let the image of Atlantis and some subtle spiritual presence sway me. I asked Stewart to tell me more. He said he needed a photo of me.

"What does my photo have to do with this?"

He explained, "The crystal is programmed with thought based on vibrations emanating from your photo."

"Yeah. Sure."

He told me that he planned to program the crystal over the weekend. When activated, it would send me thirty million signals of every known therapy, and even some unknown ones. I was more than a bit skeptical—never having heard of such a thing. Nor did I know then about the way Silicon Valley stores huge amounts of data on "chips," or wafers, thinly sliced from large silicon crystals. Inert forms are indeed part of the whole universe and are alive, intelligent, and responsive.

And then also, some Spirit Guide kept prodding me by inserting the thought, "The crystal is really very good, very, very good." I mailed Stewart my photo the next day and promptly forgot about it.

That weekend, I was strolling down a street in Ginza, the Fifth Avenue of Tokyo, when suddenly, something shifted. A second before, I was tired from the heat and weighed down by months of depression, and the next second the whole area not only sparkled, but also seemed crystal clear—light in both senses of the word, and almost translucent. If there was an "I" in that experience, it was quite luminous and melting in sweetness.

A second before, I was tired from the heat and months of depression, and the next second the whole area not only sparkled, but also seemed crystal clear....

I immediately started checking my reality systems, and wondered how such a change was possible, when, suddenly, I thought, "Of course—the crystal!" Excited, but still a bit skeptical, for my ego was struggling to regain its control of my Being. The more I thought about it though, the more excited I became.

Even now, quite a few years later, I tend to swing between two paradigms, one based upon my conventional, ego-driven upbringing, and one based upon a lighter, more optimistic version of reality.

On that day in Tokyo my soul was moving back and forth between reason and bliss. Yet here was an incontrovertible fact: Stewart had said that he intended to work on it that weekend, and here I was walking on the very Sunday he must have been programming it. I couldn't imagine any other reason for the heavenly feeling I was experiencing in a neighborhood not known for its tranquility.

Looking back now, I have to smile. Reason is a useful tool, but it rarely is the source of bliss, and its only defense against bliss is to explain it away. And then there was this kind, Indian-sounding voice in my head, saying, "The crystal is very good." At the time I wondered if it was Maharishi's voice, or possibly Babaji's voice? Anyway, at that point I decided that whatever genius was responsible for this crystal invention; I wanted to study with him.

"That can be arranged," Stewart proclaimed when I finally met him for the first time, a week after his initial phone call. He was medium tall, with dark curly hair, a prominent nose and deep-set, dark eyes—handsome, but still an ordinary enough looking representative of the species *homo sapiens*. What did I expect? Feathery protuberances on his shoulders? He had a great sense of humor, yet he was not silly and indeed had a no-nonsense side with solid judgment implied in everything he said. He was the kind of alpha male, whom one either liked or disliked. I chose to like him.

When we met, he scanned my body visually and told me which chakras were imbalanced and which organs were likely malfunctioning as a result. And each diagnostic comment he made resonated deeply with me—he was right. He knew about my uterine problems without my saying anything. Of course, I hadn't shared such intimate information with someone I hardly knew, let alone a man. Yet he knew that area was the source of my weakness, and, in 1987, that was impressive.

Through Stewart, I began corresponding with the "English School," which he sometimes referred to as "Arcadia." That name had a nice classical ring. Back then, I didn't think to ask why the School was also called Arcadia. Maybe it simply referred to the School's location in a rural part of England?

When I asked Stewart about the roots of the School, he said he didn't know. When I pressed him for more information he said he thought the School's founders were channeling and that one of their sources was ancient Tibetan Buddhism. A few weeks later Arcadia sent me a small white stone, which even now emits heat and dances in my hand.

It was to be six years before I met the Seraph who unlocked many secrets for me, including those related to the white stone.

England—My First Visit

The location of the English School in Yeovil, England was close to a famous old town called Glastonbury, considered to be the Holy Land of England—an area imbued with magical enchantment. Glastonbury is at the heart of both Arthurian and Christian legends. The supposed graves of the legendary King Arthur and Queen Guinevere were found near the abbey grounds almost a thousand years ago.

Also on the abbey grounds Christians claim that Saint Joseph of Arimathea, an uncle of Jesus, had built a church of wood and wattles shortly after the crucifixion. According to legend he was a tin merchant who traded between Judea and Cornish miners. He later became a missionary and came back to Glastonbury, where he planted his staff on the grounds of what is today Glastonbury Abbey. The staff miraculously started to bloom, and to this day a tree that once grew in Palestine still lives on the Abbey grounds.

Of all the treasures in Glastonbury, the idea that the Holy Grail may be buried there has tantalized most. St. Joseph is said to have brought to England the cup used in the Last Supper, which thereafter held the blood of Christ as it dripped from the cross. Legend has it that the cup was buried with St. Joseph on Chalice Hill, somewhere between Glastonbury's prominent hill, called the Tor, and the Abbey.

Courtesy Eastman Kodak

In 1997, on my first trip to England, I stopped off in Glastonbury and spent an afternoon exploring the ruins of the abbey, awed by the beauty of the place. I had never seen a ruined cathedral before. The abbey roof was completely missing, but the sidewalls were still standing. The windows were simply framed pictures of the sky and trees. Beneath my feet the grass was luxuriantly green and kept beautifully clipped. There was stillness in the air that spoke of hidden energies. Enhanced by the absence of visitors that day, the solitude was almost palpable.

Even before my arrival, my visit to Glastonbury had been magical. I had left London only a few days earlier on an open rail ticket and had spent an afternoon touring Stonehenge, soaking in its beautiful energies. Then I connected with my Higher Self and available Spirit Guides to plan the rest of my journey. I wanted to be in Glastonbury the following day to meet the co-founder of Arcadia, to learn more about the demise of the School. Since she was still distressed over the loss of her partner, I concluded that their relationship was about the only thing that had kept the School together.

I knew nothing about the geography or history of England except for snippets I had learned in America. When I completed my tour of Stonehenge, I asked Spirit where to go next. I was told to get back on the southbound train and to disembark at Bath.

When I arrived there, it became clear why they had led me to that particular town. It seemed that my Guides were treating me to an unusual scene in the middle of England that was so unlike any other English town. The Romans had originally built the town, and their buildings were still intact.

The Romans chose the site because of its natural hot spring. Even today the center of the town features an almost perfectly preserved ancient Roman bathhouse, with the water still gurgling up inside. Bath also has an equally well-preserved collection of Georgian buildings, and all this is rolled into one enchanted village, with period shops selling antiques and curios. Thrilled, I walked around Bath with its many unique surprises until the soft glow of the summer twilight faded into darkness. It was almost ten o'clock.

I was due in Glastonbury the next day and realized that the train did not go there. Before retiring I arranged for bus transport. The following morning I boarded the bus early. The trip was over two hours long. Driving through the village centers along the way, the bus picked up passengers at many old, quaint English towns. As soon as the bus rolled into the main street of a town called Wells, close to the end of the trip, my normal thinking processes were suddenly and completely overwhelmed by a powerful energy that flushed down through my head and then quickly surged through my entire body.

My normal thinking processes were suddenly and completely overwhelmed by a powerful energy that flushed down through my head.

My immediate impression was that every cell of my body was responding to the visual stimuli of that main street whose shops have remained unchanged for more than a thousand years. It was akin to the instant recognition of meeting a soul mate for the first time (if you have had that experience). My breathing was momentarily suspended as a flood of feelings surfaced. If I had never heard of reincarnation, I probably would have been puzzled by the experience. But since I already believed in reincarnation, I assumed that the experience indicated I had lived in Wells some time prior to this lifetime.

Later, the Seraph confirmed this impression, but on my first visit to England he was letting me naturally enjoy the reconnections without requiring reflective thinking. My experiences in England were like a moveable feast of beauty and spiritual intrigue from the moment I left London.

When the bus turned down a second street in the heart of Wells, the same energy flush repeated, as if to confirm my idea of a past life there. To date, this is the only experience I have had like this; although I always felt it odd how quickly I learned to speak Japanese during my first stay in Japan.

On arrival at Glastonbury, the bus dropped me off in front of a "Healing Store." Written clearly on a sign facing the street was a message stating that the store was devoted to spiritual healing. Since I had some time before my arranged luncheon, I walked inside to share my recent healing experiences with whoever might be there. The owner, a pleasant-looking woman in her forties, greeted me and inquired if I was planning to stay a few days in Glastonbury and where I might be staying. When I confessed I had no reservations but wanted to stay overnight, she insisted on helping me. With a skillful air, she phoned a place in town that she said was perfect for my first visit, as long as I was willing to stay at least three nights. I agreed and was pleased to find myself booked at the Chalice Well's Inn, just below the Tor, the famous hill on the edge of town.

When I got to the Inn I sensed the sacredness of the site, with its lovely gardens and fountains. I felt truly privileged to be able to stay on such hallowed grounds. Reputedly the water from Chalice Well has magical healing powers, and in the area of the Well I felt little beings, maybe fairies, dancing about. Unlike day visitors to Chalice Well's Garden, guests at the Inn had twenty-four hour access to the Well. Whenever I had the chance I made the most of this blessing by meditating in an alcove just beside this sacred place.

A former student of the English School recently told me a story for which this same area had provided the beautiful setting. One may well imagine how the following took place. One day, probably in 1986, Mark Byrnbridge, the School's co-founder, while visiting Glastonbury Abbey and lulled by its somnolent beauty, fell asleep on the grounds. Almost like Rip Van Winkle, he awoke a different man—not older, but wiser. While he slept a huge amount of esoteric information had been made available to him, apparently unlocked by the energies of Glastonbury Abbey. (To this day, this particular individual detests the word "channeling." Maybe the spirit worlds knowing his prejudice took his little nap as an opportunity to feed him information in the only way palatable to him—in the dream state.)

My visit to Glastonbury was ten years after Mark had had this experience. Thinking back to that earlier time when I was a student of Arcadia, I wasn't informed enough to know that the School's purpose had never really been all that spiritual. Furthermore, being located in Tokyo, I had only the haziest idea of what the English School was about, which was also being filtered by Stewart's experiences and explanations. The School's written materials occasionally used semi-spiritual terminology to obscure the lines between two healing modalities, allopathic medicine and spirituality—possibly to impress people, like me, who were reassured when something was clad in spiritual garb. For instance, the School once wrote to me that I had an enlightened "ally" in my aura that was confusing my self-testing of my advancement through the School's ranks. Stewart had to tell me that the word "ally" was the School's equivalent of "spirit guide." What follows is another example of the School's esoteric style:

> "The First Path is when the 1st and 7th chakras, instead of each spinning in two opposite directions around one linear axis, begin to spin in two opposite directions around a spherical axis. Also, the idasic signals become active. These signals enable active intent to be contained in inorganic structures." [p. 33, *The Way of Life*, c. 1987]

I guess the School's leaders were making the whole experience appear as scientific and rational as possible to bring on board skeptics of the healing claims they made. By blurring the distinctions between medical terminology and spirituality, they were making their teachings attractive to spiritual seekers, like me—as well as the skeptics.

I must say, though, their crystals, stones, symbols and expensive paraphernalia were intriguing. Arcadia had established powerful "crystal rooms" in countries where it had strong active centers, including in Japan, where Stewart was the leader. These rooms contained large crystals placed in sacred formations that stepped down the School's energies for use in the local area. I remember seeing huge waist-high Brazilian quartz crystals that were part of Stewart's crystal room. At the time I knew little about the purpose of their careful placement or the reason why they took up a whole room in his home. Stewart was always secretive.

Only a few years ago I learned that the most important crystal rooms were in three island countries—Japan, New Zealand and England, all off the coast of three major continents. The triangulation that resulted among these countries covered the Earth, exponentially increasing the energies. Again when talking about crystals, island countries, two of which are prone to frequent volcanic activity; there is something of the flavor of Atlantis implied.

Although the English School retained my allegiance for a long time, when one is a spiritual seeker there can be many detours, dead ends, and even dangers on the path. The School's way felt like a holding pattern, or a slight detour for me. When the School folded, it may have been a blessing in that it allowed us all to move on.

The spiritual seeker, though, has to be careful not to be swayed by seemingly spiritual organizations that have entirely different and much darker agendas. Such groups can appear harmless, and well meaning to their participants until such a point when the student wishes to move on to something else. That is when things can get unpleasant and downright dangerous.

There are no foolproof ways of recognizing such organizations. Usually such groups only get branded with the odious word "cult" after a member has died in suspicious circumstances. But there are a few indicators that one can be alert to. Be guarded if the organization requires that you sell most of your possessions and donate the funds to the group, or the organization has very high entrance and yearly maintenance fees. Also be wary if the group adheres to strict behavioral rules that set the individual apart from friends and relatives to the point that the individual loses connection with those outside the group. The old biblical saying "Ye shall know them by their fruits," (Matthew 7:16) certainly applies to any group one might be thinking of joining. Find out if the members are leading normal, happy lives as part of the larger community.

I have been asked on several occasions to help with restoring the well-being to individuals who have tried to disengage from deceptive groups. Frequently, once they leave the group nothing untoward happens until about two years after they have left. This is done to throw them off the track, and cover the behavior of the group that is still ongoing and recruiting new members. I have found that at the two year point the hooks begin to really do their damage, and the person's health deteriorates "for no apparent reason," and they start to get panic attacks, insomnia and depression.

If they are lucky enough to find me, or somebody like me, then we can help clear them of all chording to the offending group, give them ways to cleanse on their own, and keep permanently protected. Towards the end of this book there is a whole chapter devoted to this topic.

Meanwhile, the reader can meander with me along the path that I was about to explore when I landed in California in 1994.

PART II

THE SERAPH'S TEACHING

The Atlantean Connection

After spending eight years as a contented expatriate, I found myself back in California in February of 1994. America no longer felt like home. I had lived in so many places around the States: New York City, my birthplace and site of my childhood years; Maryland, close to the nation's capital for my high school and college years; Honolulu for graduate school; then the California Redwoods; Santa Barbara; San Francisco; Iowa for my doctorate; Cambridge, Massachusetts, working at Harvard; and now finally Berkeley, California, home of America's great radical university. With the exception of Hawaii, none had stirred within me a desire to belong.

In any case, I felt it was time to become re-acquainted with my birth country. I was perched at the edge of the continent, however, ready to take flight at a moment's notice. I soon discovered that I had picked the worst place for my newfound profession of psychic counselor and past-life reader. I had landed right in the middle of alternative-culture country where every other person was either a psychic or a massage therapist. It was definitely a case of bringing coals to Newcastle. I had also arrived during one of the worst recessions in the nation's history—with California being one of the states hardest hit. I couldn't even find work as a temporary typist—something I had done in the past as a last resort.

I finally discovered that by advertising nationally as well as locally, I could eke out a living. I kept my expenses down by using a bicycle as my only form of transportation.

Also, I had expanded my repertoire of abilities. By 1994 I could perceive whether a person's soul was depressed within minutes of speaking to them, whether by phone or in person, even if they appeared to be cheerful. I wouldn't just diagnose an individual's core problem; I had also learned to relieve it through remedies devised by my Spirit Guides. Occasionally, I used my personal hands-on healing ability, which gradually grew stronger over the years.

Thus my work was sufficiently original to allow me to hold a special niche in California's psychic community. Maybe Spirit had arranged my re-location to America's shores for some reason. ***But what was that reason?***

True, by April I had already lectured about my past-life soul work at the San Francisco Whole Life Expo and felt blessed that 125 people attended my lecture on a normal workday. Even though my work gave me tremendous pleasure, being in a new place starting over again was difficult. I often sat alone in my apartment, fretting about whether I was in the right place to continue my spiritual journey. And I was still very curious about the meaning of my little white stone. Since my Guides had told me that Atlantis was the key, I was on the look out for any mention of that.

One day in a local newspaper I happened to spot a free lecture entitled "Atlantean Crystal Healing." Coincidently the teacher giving the lecture had impressed me at the San Francisco Whole Life Expo. I decided to attend his lecture.

Sitting in a group of thirty people, I thought that the room felt at odds with the general feeling of New Age presentations. There were no crystals or other New Age paraphernalia in the dark meeting hall. The bearded, bespectacled presenter was speaking with what sounded like a Brooklyn accent. He told us that he had been born and raised in Mississippi, which was odd because he didn't have a Southern drawl. Perhaps his parents had been immigrants?

He introduced himself: "My name is Stanley. I was formerly an atheist and mathematics lecturer. I was forced to retire due to a debilitating illness—severe stiffness of the neck. This mysterious disease is life-threatening, and the medical profession really doesn't know how to treat it. Because I was spending most of my time in bed, I started investigating all forms of energy healing, and I found that by running energy through my body I was able to stabilize my condition. Slowly I began to recover to the point that I was functioning again. About a year later, while I was having breakfast, I literally 'saw God' in my teacup. To say the least, I was never the same after that. Instead of returning to mathematics, I have become a full-time energy healer and teacher."

Continuing, he said, "As a means of demonstrating the power of the upcoming workshop, I am going to give you a taste of the energies to be taught in it today. If you attend the workshop you will receive them permanently. For your safety, however, I have put a strong protective energy grid in this room. Therefore, when I start to run the energies through you, they are completely safe. I am now going to give you a crystal for the duration of the lecture to help you feel the energies." He passed around several beautiful quartz crystals.

"Now close your eyes, as I run the first energy."

We settled into what felt like a six-minute meditation, but must have been longer.

At the end he asked: "What did you feel?"

Someone said that the energy felt strong around his heart. Another attendee mentioned that their hands feel hot holding the crystal. I noticed that my body felt warmer and tingly when he was running the energy. What I found strange though, was that while he was supposedly sending us this energy, he simply stood at the front of the room, with eyes closed. I guess I was expecting him to be at least waving a wand. It was hard for me to believe that someone who appeared to be doing absolutely nothing was inducing all the energy I was experiencing inside. *Was this some kind of magic?*

Stanley continued with the energy transfers. After about three quarters of an hour he announced, "Let's take a break." Since he hadn't mentioned Atlantis, I approached him to ask a question.

"I have a small white stone at home that I received from an esoteric school in England about seven years ago. Can you tell me if the stone has any connection to Atlantis?"

Looking at some point above my head, he replied: "THERE IS AN ENORMOUS ANGEL STANDING BEHIND YOU."

I didn't feel anything around me. And lacking experience with angels, I couldn't imagine what this was about.

"The angel is telling me that you and I need to work together to bring out a mystery school that was known in Atlantean times."

I had only a vague idea of what he meant by the term "mystery school." Now I know that in Western culture "mystery school" refers to serious occult learning, often taking years of study, with the purpose of changing circumstances and major trends in the real world.

I wondered if this man that I assumed to be a master spiritual teacher was really asking me to partner with him, even though we had never met before. As I was witnessing all this, something shifted in me making me more receptive to what he was saying. But you might wonder why I was willing to trust a virtual stranger's assertions based upon one surprising outburst concerning a nonphysical being?

Well, I had been sitting in a room for close to an hour, in which everyone seemed to be experiencing unseen forces playing in their bodies—some felt like they were being touched, others felt great warmth, and I had felt various tingling sensations throughout. And it appeared that Stanley and I both had psychic gifts, which were being enhanced in each other's presence, probably because consciousness has a collective field effect. You tickle the person sitting next to you, and somebody across the room starts to laugh. And I confess that one other factor was at work. Since I had spent nineteen years as a university student, an environment in which ninety percent of the faculty is male, Stanley had the correct collegial, authoritative manner because he had taught at universities and he looked the part as well, being bearded and bespeckled as he was. This, I am sorry to say, still impressed me. All this resulted in my

> The Angel is telling me that you and I need to work together to bring out a mystery school that was known in Atlantean times.

concluding that Stanley was legitimate. At the time, though, I didn't reflect at all. I simply jumped in.

"I'd love to work with you," I said. "How do you propose we do this?"

"We can have sessions alternating between your home and mine, maybe twice-a-month," he says.

I was thrilled at the thought of meeting him regularly in such an open-ended project involving angels and Atlantis. It felt too good to be true. And so sudden.

"Please bring any English School materials that you still have to our first session, including the white stone. I want to see if there is anything useful in what you have," he said. "Can we first meet at my home in Oakland in a few weeks from now?"

"Sure," I replied. "I will call to get directions and arrange a time."

On the day we had planned to meet, I was bursting with anticipation. I carried my bicycle onto the train and rode it up the gradual slope to the lower Oakland hills where Stanley lived. I brought all my printed material from the English School, including my white stone.

Once I arrived, he casually looked at some of the booklets and loose writings I had brought and said: "Some of the names might be helpful, but we won't need most of this material after all."

"What about the stone?"

Oh yes. It is quite powerful. I think I could use one too."

"I really don't know how it was made," I responded.

"Don't worry; I will have the angel help me make one."

Other than the creation of his special stone, Stanley waived away all the rest of the School's paraphernalia, including many beautiful symbols and crystals. "Let's call in the angel."

"How are you going to do that?"

"Tell me again the name of the founder of the English School? I believe the angel around you is the founder's Solar Angel."

"What do you mean by 'Solar Angel'?" I asked.

"I consider that term to be a more accurate description of this type of angel than the common term 'guardian angel.' Your Solar Angel is the angel assigned to you at birth by the Solar Logos. The Solar Logos is an expression that a Tibetan spirit guide called Dwahl Kuhl used to designate the sentient being associated with the Sun, like Gaia is the sentient being associated with planet Earth."

> Your Solar Angel is the angel assigned to you at birth by the Solar Logos.

"I will now call upon the angel using the founder's name." Stanley's eyes closed to call the angel, and a moment later he confirmed the angel's presence and that we could begin.

"Please ask the angel about the Atlantean origins of the system," I requested.

"The angel is saying that the Atlanteans utilized the ideas associated with these energies as a cosmological foundation of their civilization."

I asked him to explain more. He replied that the system we were about to learn was the foundational belief system of the Atlantean worldview.

Hard to believe, but I kept silent.

"The angel is saying that in Atlantean times the system was called *Ecumatschii.*" (Eh-kyu-ma-chai)

I felt myself resisting the sound of this word. I guess I was expecting something more melodious. I felt such a weird word might detract from the future popularity of our newly planned mystery school.

"The angel is ready to transmit the first energy which will begin to open the system in our bodies." Stanley asked me to close my eyes.

Something stirred within me, beginning with a tingling in my head, which slowly descended into my chest. I felt warmth gently swirling throughout my body, especially in my hands, which grew hot. After a few minutes I noticed how drowsy and relaxed I felt.

Stanley then whispered, "The energy is now tapering off, so slowly come back and open your eyes."

I started to feel normal again.

"The angel is saying that the energy is safe and will permanently install itself in our bodies. Its purpose is to heal us through increasing pranic uptake of the food we eat, the water we drink and the air we breathe."

"What do you mean by 'pranic uptake'?"

"Prana is the Sanskrit word meaning 'life-force energy,' like the Chinese *chi* and the Japanese *ki.*"

This was my first experience with this sort of energy, which didn't remind me of anything I learned from the

English School.

Stanley suddenly blurted out: "This is the most powerful healing energy I have ever experienced—much more powerful than Reiki."

I was impressed. I knew he was a Reiki master and a former practitioner of Transcendental Meditation. Reiki is a form of energy healing that originated with a 19th century Japanese man's attempt to channel universal healing energies. He was so certain of the existence of such energies and their potential availability to mankind that he kept working with his spirit guides until he discovered the key to connecting with its source. Humanity has benefited ever since.

"It all started with T. M," Stanley said.

I started to feel closer to him when I heard this. "Ask the angel what we can do with this new energy?"

"He says that this first initiation is just a beginning to open the main energy channel of *Life-force Energy* in our bodies and that we are not meant to activate it because it is intelligent energy and will run on its own."

"Why did the energy feel dream-like as it was coming in?"

"The relaxing component of the energy is merely the experience of the carrier-wave holding the energy. It is a delivery system for the real energy contained within it, which has a self-activating, intelligent purpose."

As he spoke, I wrote down every word. At the top of the page I wrote: *"Life-force Energy Initiations."*

"The angel is now ready to give us the ability to give out this energy to other people."

"How long will that take?"

"Oh, probably another six-minutes, like the first initiation."

Closing my eyes, I felt a similar energetic bath. Following the initiation I wrote the words: *"Giving out the primary opening of Life-force Energy."*

Then the angel quickly gave us the *"secondary opening of Life-force Energy,"* which was opening the energy in all parts of our bodies. While this energy was coming in, I began to notice how clear my head had become. I felt more alert than before.

Once we received the initiation, the angel informed us:

"These energies are intelligent and work on your bodies automatically, healing various old problems."

On that first day my notes read as follows:

🌱 **The opening of the Primary Life-force Energy Channel, which mainly targets our chakras.**

🌱 **The opening of the Secondary Life-force Energy Channel, which sends energy to all parts of our bodies.**

🌱 **A Life-force Energy that enhances the functioning of our kidneys.**

🌱 **An initiation to create a Life-force Energy Channel with people and objects, such as food or crystals, to enliven them and give us much more prana.**

As the session came to a close, I noticed how lively I felt, with much more mental clarity than I'd had before. We made an appointment to meet at my apartment a few weeks later.

During the time in-between sessions I was amazed at my great energy levels. What a difference from before I began this work! I also realized that my hands no longer felt arthritic, which is something I had been concerned about.

It had been three weeks since our last meeting, and now my new colleague finally arrived at my home.

"Today, we are going to learn some amazing stuff."

He then called in the Solar Angel once more. "The angel says he wants to teach us how to empower quartz crystals with Life-force Energy energies. But first, let me teach you a technique for cleaning quartz crystal down to the atomic level."

"You mean there is a better way to clean quartz crystal than placing it in salt or salt water?"

"Yes, this is the best way I know of. Do you have some ordinary quartz crystals in the house?"

"Yes, I do."

> Let me teach you a technique for cleaning quartz crystal down to the atomic level.

"Well, please get them so I can demonstrate how this works."

I found some hidden away and brought them to him.

"Now, put the crystal in your dominant hand and simply ask your Solar Angel to clean it for you."

As I closed my palm around the small crystal and mentally called upon my Solar Angel, I could feel a strong vibration in my hand. After about two minutes, the teacher said, "That should be enough," and asked me for the crystal so he could test it.

"Yes, it is clean. We are ready to receive the crystal

empowerment from the angel."

After receiving the initiation, we picked up our crystals again and closed our eyes to imbue the crystals with Life-force Energy energies. I noticed how charged my crystal felt.

The angel told us that once they are charged we could wear them on our bodies for up to five hours at a time, at which point we might feel some overload from the strong energies they contain.

"How would it feel if we overloaded on the energy?"

"You might feel a bit hyperactive—as if you had drunk too much caffeine."

During this second session, as Stanley received information about the energies from the angel, I studiously recorded every word:

🌱 Ability to empower quartz crystals with Life-force Energy.

🌱 Ability to energize a room or house with a Life-force Energy grid.

🌱 Ability to do hands-on healing of self and others.

Once the angel gave us the initiation for the energy grid, Stanley asked me to put the grid into my apartment immediately. While I was sending out the energy, he said: "I can see lines of light going in all directions." The energy coming out of my hands felt very powerful, and I could feel a real shift around my body too.

> I can see lines of light going in all directions.

"Where do you think it is appropriate to put the grid in the future?" I asked.

"Probably any place that needs healing and uplifting

energies. If you want to keep your favorite local restaurant in business, you might put the grid in there too."

Then we received the energy to do hands-on healing with Life-force Energy, I immediately tried to send the energy into my own body and was amazed that I could feel the energies coming through. Generally, energy healers cannot work on themselves, so when the healing energy penetrated deeply into my own body, I felt that this was a breakthrough. Straight away I gave Stanley some healing for his chronic neck condition.

"Ruth," he said, "Why don't you give out this life-force energy with every soul reading you do?" My past-life readings had evolved into "Soul Readings" by then.

"That's a good idea," I responded. Then, I implored him to ask the angel more about the Atlantean connection.

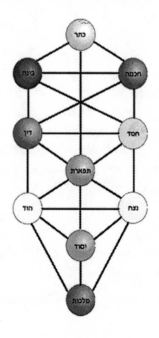

"I am getting an image similar to the Tree-of-Life." He was referring to the famous image from the ancient Jewish Kabbalah that doesn't look like a real tree, but is a type of diagram incorporating ten interlocking centers. The energy waveforms we were receiving did resemble the Kabbalah *sephirot*, or the 'fruits' on the Tree-of-Life.

Stanley continued: "Just as the Tree-of-Life, the Ecumatschii system also has ten major waveforms, or energies. Over time, the angel will tell us about the rest of them."

"Does this mean that the system has some connection to the Kabbalah too?" I asked.

"Not necessarily," he said. "The Kabbalistic Tree-of-Life is actually a rough diagram of an energy transformer, with the top centers acting to step down God's powerful energies into smaller portions that humans can handle. Although similar to the sephirot of the tree of life, the energies we are receiving from the angel are unique." Stanley further explained: "We can call them 'waveforms.' The term 'waveform' denotes that they are both energy and sacred geometric form. These two views are different ways of describing the universe, with neither ultimately being truer than the other. We can explain universal energies in terms of geometry (every energy has an underlying geometric structure which gives rise to it) or we can explain geometry in terms of energy (a geometric form acquires its powers and properties through holding energy in a certain way)."

Later, I found out that Stanley had slightly spiritualized what quantum physicists refer to as "wave-particle duality,"— the belief that light and matter both exhibit properties of waves and particles.

Each time Stanley and I met; there was the excitement of having the angel's energy around us. In-between our meetings I was regularly giving out the healing energies to all my friends and relatives who were willing to be guinea pigs. I also set up a free Friday clinic in my home and advertised publicly. A few people always showed up each Friday, and I had several success stories.

The first one I remember was Stephanie, who met me at a psychic fair with her husband. She was walking with crutches, as she had recently broken a small critical bone in her foot. She told me that if the bone didn't set properly in the next month she was going to need an operation. She wanted to know if I could guarantee that the Life-force Energy would heal her foot properly without the operation. I said I didn't know, but I was willing to treat her at no cost. She came to me each Friday for about two months. At the end of that time, her doctor gave her the all clear, as the bone had healed properly. She was grateful.

In the San Francisco Bay area there is a large gay population and AIDS is prevalent. I had one client with AIDS who came to see me regularly and claimed that I was helping him greatly.

Within a year and a half, Stanley and I received five major waveforms, or branches of the system. The angel told us that there was a logical sequence to learning the system, and that is how he was presenting the energies to us. Much later I was able to see the logic. Even in the beginning, I saw that the Life-force Energy was about healing the body physically, and the second energy waveform, which we dubbed the Harmony Waveform, was about healing the emotional body.

After receiving each initiation, which generally took six minutes, the angel told us telepathically what the energy was for. In this way we received many "angelic downloads." Once the energies were permanently installed in our bodies, the angel told us that we could call them up at will.

One day I received a call from my mentor.

"I am sorry, Ruthie, but I am not going to continue to work with you on the system."

"What!? Why not?"

"My schedule is too full, and I have many other new energies that I am working with."

I was incredulous. Although it had become noticeably difficult recently to schedule our meetings, I didn't understand how he could be saying this, when he often repeated that this was the most powerful energy he had ever experienced!

"What about the mystery school we were going to found together?" Almost emotionless he said: "My Guides have informed me that all along these energies were really meant for your growth, and not mine. Also they said that you have probably received enough of the energies for this lifetime."

> My Guides have informed me that all along these energies were really meant for your growth, and not mine.

"Is it okay then for me to continue to give out the energies and possibly teach them one day?"

"Sure, you can use them." And with that, our conversation ended, and I was left in shock.

Although I may never completely understand why he did this, I took his words at face value. I saw him a few times after that, but we didn't discuss the issue. I remain grateful for his assistance in my spiritual development.

Soon after that, I realized that I had been passively receiving the energies and information from him all along, feeling that I had little expertise to contribute to the process. Now the only way to continue working with the angel was through using my own psychic tool, the pendulum, and the unique powers of attracting the angel that appeared to be associated with my white stone. *Were these two small stones adequate for the task?*

The Seraph

Two weeks after my mentor quit, I felt it was time to try communicating with the angel on my own. With my pendulum in my right hand, I centered myself and began swinging the small stone attached to its silver chain. I know how the pendulum normally feels, but now it was taking on a life of its own as it whirled clockwise through the air pulling my right hand with it. I realized the angel was signaling me that he was willing to work with me. I was strangely moved. A few tears welled up in my eyes.

With my eyes half-closed, I said out loud "I call upon Mark Byrnbridge's Solar Angel to please come to me now." Suddenly the angel arrived and gave me a start.

Right before my eyes in large bold letters, a strange but beautiful name appeared floating in mid-air. Could this actually be his real name?

> Right before my eyes in large bold letters, a strange but beautiful name appeared floating in mid-air.

That's the only thing it can be—I thought—I have never seen anything like this in my life. Being strongly *clairsentient*—the psychic gift of feeling vibrations, but barely *clairvoyant*—the psychic gift of vision, I rarely saw things. I knew the angel must have been doing this.

As I tentatively began to pronounce his name, I loved the way it sounded. Then the pendulum started whirling around to my right indicating his strong approval of my pronunciation. His name is not difficult for an English speaker to say, but was unknown to me.

"What sort of angel are you? I don't recognize your name."

"I am a Seraph."

Not quite believing this, I rephrased the question. "Do you mean that you are one of the highest angels in the universe?"

"Yes."

Suddenly the idea that the California teacher mentioned, that the reason we had worked together was for my development not his, began to make sense. I was being given new, privileged information that superseded what I had previously learned. This angel informed me that he had never been anyone's Solar Angel. He merely went along with the mistake that my recent mentor made when calling upon him in this way.

For a while I openly shared the Seraph's name with my students. Then one day, after my students left I felt the Seraph demanding my attention.

"What's the matter?" I asked him.

"You are not to share my name with others."

"Why not?"

"I do not want everyone to know about me."

"I don't want to draw attention to myself because those who practice the dark arts can seek ways of neutralizing Me."

I was surprised, to say the least, by the angel's fear of exposure. Since generally we bandy about the names of the archangels, I assumed that angels were invincible. Here the Seraph was showing me that he needed some protection.

Later I discovered why.

The Seraph's Teaching

Once I had established a high-quality connection with the Seraph, I set myself the task of channeling the next major seraphic energy. I knew the name of the subsequent waveform, and was sure that it was related to consciousness. The notion of expanding consciousness had been central to the Transcendental Meditation teaching with which I was so familiar. Maharishi had certain memorable sayings like "Knowledge is structured in consciousness" and "Knowledge is different in different states of consciousness." He also taught Sanskrit phrases like *"yogastah kurukarmani"* which means "Established in Being, perform action." Such ideas deeply resonated with me, as transcendental consciousness was really part of my makeup in those days.

Therefore I was excited that the next waveform was to be about consciousness. On the day I was guided to attempt my first channeling of the Seraph I sat on my bed, took the phone off the hook, and began writing notes to identify what initiations might be part of this new waveform. Slowly, through my pendulum, the Seraph indicated to me when my ideas were on track. This is the list of initiations that I generated that first day:

Expansion of Consciousness Waveform

- ❧ Expansion of Consciousness Channel Opening
- ❧ DNA attunement—to fine-tune the energy in the body
- ❧ Reversal of ageing initiation
- ❧ Wish Fulfillment (to be activated)
- ❧ Pituitary Attunement—the main organ to focus on for this energy
- ❧ Soma/Bliss attunement (to be activated once a day)
- ❧ Meditation Enhancement (to be activated before meditating)

Then I asked the Seraph to download the individual energies into my own consciousness. With each installation I could feel the neuronal pathways being activated as the energy streamed into my body.

When completed, I felt strongly empowered. Now I knew I was able to channel the remaining waveforms of the system.

The next question became how I was to pass the system on to others. I had already been using Life-force Energy and the Harmony Waveform healing in my free clinic, with clients in person, and over the phone. I wondered what the best format to spread this exciting new process might be. Stanley and I had held four-hour sessions together. With our monthly meetings, though, it took us a year and a half to get through only half of the system.

One of my clients suggested that the best format might be a series of all-day workshops. That tantalized me. People have so little time these days, that any way to speed up the process would be helpful. Although there were problems in fitting all the material into one-day sessions, I decided upon the workshop format.

Next, the system needed a name. The first name that I thought of was "Atlantean Angel Healing." I leafleted all of Berkeley announcing my new workshop with that name, and held my first course in my apartment in 1996. Eight people attended.

One was Bonnie, a pretty, young suburban mother with two small children. A former computer programmer, she was now a Feng Shui consultant. Bonnie was attracted to the workshop because of the "Atlantean" connection. After the workshop, she mentioned how much she loved the energies as they were coming in. She tended to see vivid colors associated with the energies. Bonnie has turned out to be one of the most devoted practitioners of the Seraphim energies.

Lindsay was an electrician with a keen interest in politics and esoteric spirituality. We had met at a psychic fair a few months earlier, and he really enjoyed discussing these subjects. He and another close male friend were part of that first workshop. Another student, Maureen, often felt spirits around her and wanted to know more about them. In her seventies, she wanted help in healing various ailments that had cropped up in her life before the course. Maureen found that once she began the work she had much more energy, and her back gave her fewer problems. She became a devoted student.

Carlos, a Mexican-American, was a bit lost but found comfort in receiving the energies. Psychically I discovered that he is really an angel in a human body. Such people tend to be a bit ungrounded. He attended all four levels of the system as it evolved in Berkeley.

This same group followed my work for the next five years and completed the eighth waveform on the five-year anniversary of their Level 1 workshop. Teaching these students took longer than I had hoped, but I was happy channeling the new waveforms at this leisurely pace and told my students that I wanted the system to unfold organically.

In 1998 I returned to Australia for the first time since 1993. It was a bittersweet return as I tried to reconnect with people I had known in the early nineties and who had moved on with their lives. Australia was famous for its 'larrikins' who sometimes lived off the public largesse even though they probably were able to do some type of work.

In the early nineties with about ten percent of the population on semi-permanent vacation, it was easy to visit with friends in the middle of a weekday and have a 'cuppa,' enjoying Australia's beautiful sunshine, flora and fauna. The ambience in Sydney in those days contrasted with my previous experiences in America where work was central to everyone's sense of self-worth, and friends rarely met. Instead of meeting face-to-face they tended to be satisfied with long telephone conversations. I definitely preferred the more laid-back Aussie lifestyle.

In any case, by 1998 American influence on the Australian work ethic had taken its toll. In just five years there was a much higher employment rate, and my former carefree friends now had full-time jobs.

In the intervening years my focus on spirituality had taken me further from the popular Australian pub scene than ever. Still, during that first visit back to Sydney, I longed to revive my former life there. Therefore, when the Sydney

Mind Body Spirit Festival invited me to speak at the November 1998 Festival, I was delighted to accept.

When I returned to Sydney that Southern summer, my talk was entitled "Angel Healing." On that occasion, the hall overflowed, and people even sat in the aisles. The crowd loved the Seraph's energies. About fifty people signed up for a full-day workshop the following weekend.

> The crowd loved the Seraph's energies.

I rented a hall in Bondi Junction not far from the famous Bondi Beach. On the day of the course the attendees were passionate about the energies.

Afterward they asked me what else they could learn while I was still in Australia. Their enthusiasm prompted me to say, without prior consideration: "I guess the Seraph could make some of you teachers. How many would be interested?"

About thirty people raised their hands. I hadn't given any thought to this possibility. Then and there, I picked a date for the first Teacher Training workshop—a one-day course. The Seraph gave his full blessing to this new development.

I was staying in a spacious Darlinghurst penthouse at the time, and the following week thirty students crowded into my main lounge. We began the first teacher-training course for what I was then calling "Angel Healing—Level 1."

Following this course, the students wanted to begin Level 2 of the system, and attendance at that course was also large. By the time I returned to America five months later, most of the group had become teachers up through Level 3. They were awed by their experiences with the energies and were ready to soak up anything the Seraph wanted to share.

This was the beginning of my being torn between the U.S. and Australia, as I had begun to put down roots in California. At the time, there were two things keeping me in Berkeley—my beloved Dutch rabbit companion and my close friend Clare.

Clare not only shared my passions for knowledge and spirituality, she actually had *time* to spend with me. Her situation was unique, however. She was independently wealthy, plus she chose not to work. In America even the wealthy often work because they want to fit into a culture where work defines one's identity.

From 1998 until 2001 I traveled between America and Australia sometimes twice a year. I couldn't make up my mind about which country to call 'home.' Four years of indecision were taking its toll on me, however, and I knew I had to decide soon, as I felt my life was on hold.

What are Seraphim?

Since the 2000 Olympics, more people probably have a sense of what Sydney is like. Even though it's one of the world's most beautiful cities, its beauty is hard to capture in a postcard. I remember seeing many images of the Opera House before I arrived the first time, and thought what's the big deal? This is one case, though, where no amount of imagery can capture the beauty of this place.

When I arrived back in Sydney, now intending to stay, my Australian friends and students welcomed and supported me. Some had already taken the Seraphim system into a new direction. One of the first things we did was to pick a good name for the practice. The Seraph strongly urged us to have one that included the word "seraphim." After months of toying with various names we settled on the term "Seraphim Blueprint."

Then one of my students, who had become a teacher of the system, suggested that I should write a book about the Seraphim Blueprint as an aid to explaining it. I realized she was right and thought about the fastest way to do this.

Channeling the Seraph in front of my students with a tape recorder proved to be the best approach. Still, I never grasped how much work writing a book was, no matter what shortcuts I took.

As part of this process I first researched the terms 'angels' and 'seraphim,' thus discovering the 'science of angels' or 'angelology.' I quickly saw that some reference works took angels seriously while others did not. The Catholic Encyclopedia has a long article on 'seraphim,' while the Britannica's coolness to the subject limits its article to the *belief* in angels, with almost no specific mention of seraphim.

Although many cultures discuss nonphysical beings, the biblical concept of "angel" has its roots in ancient Babylonia, where the Jewish people absorbed numerous concepts while they were exiled in that empire more than 2,500 years ago.

In the Old Testament, the Hebrew term for angels is *mal'akhim*. The English word 'angel' derives from the Greek word *angelos*. In all three languages the meaning is *'messenger' of God*. The biblical authors apparently assumed that their readership already knew about angels, because the references to them are brief with little mention of their essential nature.

From various references to angels in the Judeo-Christian tradition we know that the Old Testament mentions two types—Seraphim and Cherubim. According to Judaism, God created angels on the second day of creation, as the first intelligent beings in the universe, unable to procreate, but granted immortality.

In the Bible some angels exhibit divine qualities and some exhibit human qualities. Although angels are not infallible, their actions are closer to perfection than ours. They appear to have emotions and free will as we do. They worship God and are capable of love. With immense power and influence on Earth, angels play many roles, from carrying out God's judgment to advancing our personal and spiritual growth. With the passage of time, Western cultures have tended to exalt angels more, giving them a status closer to the glory of God.

Over the millennia, though, there has been a waxing and waning of interest in angels. Appearing sporadically throughout the Old Testament, angels first became prevalent in the Jewish tradition at the time of the great crises occurring to the Hebrews from about 200 B.C. to 100 A.D. When in the Middle East various competing empires were on the road of conquest, they almost always swept through Judea due to its position linking Europe, Africa and Asia. This began the long tradition of Jewish suffering that had everything to do with location, location, location.

The rabbis in this time of continued crisis were uncomfortable with the independent power attributed to angels, since the major premise of Judaism is that God is One. Thus, they began to suppress the interest in angels by removing texts full of angelic references from the approved list of biblical lore.

Christians are responsible for keeping the angelic teachings intact, resulting in their preservation. Influenced by the angelology of Jewish sects, such as the Pharisees and the Essenes, as well as the then current angelology of the Hellenistic world, the early Christians further enhanced and developed theories and beliefs in angels and demons beyond the scant references to angels in the Old Testament. In the New Testament, celestial beings were grouped into seven ranks: Angels, Archangels, Principalities, Powers, Virtues, Dominions, and Thrones. The Old Testament Cherubim and Seraphim were added to the above seven ranks, and thus there were nine choirs of angels in later Christian mystical theology.

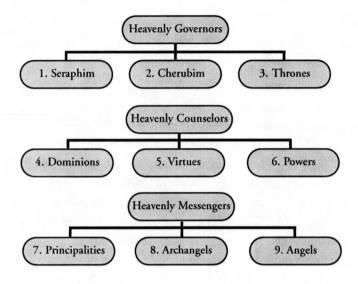

According to tradition the two lowest orders of angels, the angels and archangels, assisted humanity, while the top orders were to commune mainly with God and fulfill more cosmic purposes.

Until the Dark Ages, Christians often called upon angelic assistance. When the plague occurred, resulting in the deaths of one out of four Europeans, they began to feel that the angels had forsaken them, and appreciation of angels waned.

One of the reasons for the recent revival of interest in angels is the creation, in the spirit of the 1960's, of many alternate avenues of communicating with the divine that obviate the need for assistance from traditional religious authority. With the public's recent avid interest in angels, many new stories of their presence proliferated. And the angels have responded with stronger physical indications of their company, rewarding those humans who have taken notice of them.

Angels have sometimes appeared in modern times even to

highly skeptical people in order to prevent a tragedy, and occasionally they have taken on human form. There is the well-known instance referred to as the "Angels of Mons" that occurred in an early World War I battle. Two British divisions held off an attack at Mons, Belgium by six German divisions, even though they were so outnumbered. The British were gradually forced to retreat, but with much fewer casualties than was expected. Exhausted through lack of sleep, British troops reported that a host of angels appeared in the sky seemingly on the Allied side, which they believed helped them retreat with fewer losses. Two years later German prisoners of war said they had indeed seen angel-like bright lights hovering in the sky above the hill that separated them from the British, and they reported that they seemed powerless to advance. The passage of time has made some sources questionable, but respected historians have noted the incident as real.

I recall being amazed by the experience reported by Pierre Jovanovic, a French news reporter, of an angelic intervention when he was based in Los Angeles. In 1988 while riding as a passenger in a car on a California freeway, an invisible force suddenly threw him across the seat. A second later a bullet whizzed through the spot where he had been sitting. He realized that there was no plausible explanation for his being saved from a drive-by shooting other than spiritual intervention. Although agnostic until then, he spent the next few years researching angels and then wrote an authoritative book about them, *An Inquiry into the Existence of Guardian Angels: A Journalist's Investigative Report.*

While riding as a passenger in a car on a California freeway, an invisible force suddenly threw him across the seat.

In my angel research I discovered the Hebrew term *"seraphim"* is a masculine, plural word. The Seraph I had been interacting with does come across as being powerful and masculine. The word "seraph" is a composite of two meanings—*"ser"* meaning "higher being," or "guardian angel," and *"rapha"* meaning "healer, "doctor, or "surgeon." In the Bible they are referred to as "the fiery ones" burning up in their love of God. As they were further elaborated upon in Christian theology, Seraphim are beings of pure light and have direct communication with God. Their element of fire symbolically represents both purification and love.

The prophet Isaiah provides one of the best descriptions of the Seraphim standing behind the Throne of God in Isaiah 6:2: "Above it [the throne] stood the seraphim: each one had six wings; with twain he covered his face, and with twain he covered his feet, and with twain he did fly."

Isaiah says that these angels call to one another: "Holy, Holy, Holy is the Lord of hosts; the whole earth is full of His Glory." This well-known phrase has been given the code name of "Trisagion."

There is little else in the Bible explaining seraphim. And since Biblical times, mention of this order of angels is rare. Thus it is commonly thought that archangels are the highest order of angels. Actually they are the highest order whose sole purpose is to assist humanity.

The Seraph told me that if I hadn't met him in 1994, the order of Seraphim might have continued to be only referred to in obscure articles written in encyclopedias. It had become time for the Seraphim to be more involved in our lives. But after doing my homework on angels, I was still puzzled by such a high angel seeking me out of all the light-workers on the planet. ***Why me?***

The Seraph Answers

In planning this book, I was hoping that the entire process would take a few afternoons of channeling the Seraph in front of my students. Because I felt the Seraph's information was so important, I wanted it to be birthed quickly.

Since I had no previous experience channeling, I realized this was my chance to test both my latent channeling abilities as well as the Seraph's ability to use me as a spokeswoman. The Seraph supported my idea of going into a light trance to channel him with the help of my pendulum. Never one to avoid challenges, I set a date, invited my students to attend, and hoped it went to plan.

The day we picked for the first session was in January 2002—the New Year being auspicious for new beginnings. Ten students excitedly arrived in my lounge. I held my pendulum in my right hand and the white stone in my left to make a stronger connection with the Seraph.

To get us in the mood, I had the group exchange testimonials regarding Seraphim energies and then invited the Seraph to join us in a preparatory meditation. Following the meditation I had my students open their eyes to become alert, while I kept my eyes closed; for I now planned to stay in a meditative space while they asked the Seraph questions, and we waited for his response.

Questions and Answers

I let the brave ones take turns, while I waited for the Seraph's response. As I slowly spoke within the light trance, I concentrated on discerning correct responses by feeling which way my pendulum was turning. Even with my eyes closed I was familiar with the pendulum's patterns and was able to distinguish how well I was attuned to the Seraph's energies. If the pendulum turned clockwise that meant the Seraph agreed with my spoken explanation. If I wasn't on track, the pendulum swung counter-clockwise.

Within the answers the Seraph occasionally took over my speech without letting me filter his words. Whenever he did this, his words are italicized. While channeling him, my voice and mannerisms only changed slightly. His speech was more clipped, to the point and more serious than my own.

Session 1–27th January 2002

Can you please explain how the Seraphim energies originated? And was God directly involved in the creation process?

The system was created by thirteen Seraphim, thirteen thousand years ago. Galactic need created the energies for many beings throughout the galaxy. The timing of the creation was important for our galaxy, but not specifically for this planet. Eighteen thousand different planets in the galaxy have used these energies. That means there are 18,000 civilizations in the galaxy that are advanced enough to use the system. The total number of intelligent systems in the galaxy is about 40,000. Referring to your question about God, we could say that God is more of a principle, rather than a being. I am saying that God already acts through the Seraphim, having previously delegated tasks to them within our galaxy.

The system was created by thirteen Seraphim, thirteen thousand years ago.

If the energies are intelligent and healing, then why did the system disappear? Why did Atlantean culture disappear?

When the Seraphim created their system, Atlantis was the most vibrant culture on the planet. The introduction of these seraphic energies just happened to coincide with the existence of Atlantean culture. Although the Platonic myth of Atlantis assumed that Atlanteans were a human race, they were not quite third dimensional. The Atlanteans were fifth dimensional, with some ability to impinge on the third dimension.

What you now call the "Seraphim Blueprint" was one of several Atlantean belief systems. Atlantis existed for about 8,000 years, and these energies were introduced in the fourth millennium of their culture for roughly six hundred years. At its peak, fifty-five percent of Atlanteans used these energies. Then the ability of the Atlanteans to draw on these energies faded.

Even then, the Atlanteans, generally, didn't use the energies in the same active, conscious way as we use them today. About half of Atlanteans of that middle era were *exposed* to the energies in some form. They were merely receivers of the energy, in the same way one might receive a healing in the same way some of your friends, or children, have received healings. They didn't all channel the energies. We might draw an analogy to people going to church today. You are exposed to Christianity, or Judaism, or other religions, but you don't all practice them. You know about them, you've heard about them. In that same sense Atlanteans heard about these energies for six hundred years. Some of these people were merely receiving these energies, while others were actively channeling the energies.

Were the people that actively channelled these energies seen as a cult?

They weren't seen as a cult. Many Atlanteans were telepathic, so quite a few were interested in the energies because they felt them to be good. They didn't need as much physical proof as we do.

How can we overcome our need for physical proof?

The more you meditate, the more you shift your energy into a higher vibration, and the less you will need physical proof. You can't do this for others except in the sense that the greater the number of people who are meditating on the planet, the easier it will become for all of us to understand celestial reality—there is an effect that will be

As the population grows on the planet, the natural "wiring" of human physiology will allow for greater telepathic powers.

felt in terms of the collective consciousness on the planet. As the population grows on the planet, the natural "wiring" of human physiology will allow for greater telepathic powers. That's one *positive* outcome of over-population.

Is there a grand master plan in relation to these energies?

There is no Grand Master Plan. I am working alone. I do not have much help. The other Seraphim are gone. [He means of the original thirteen Seraphim that created the Seraphim Blueprint, thirteen thousand years ago] *I have some assistance from other angels, sixty-eight in number. I am not working with any other Seraphim. Other Seraphim have other responsibilities. There are about 140 Seraphim working with the Solar System.* [It appears that Seraphim have different assignments and probably different interests in their custodial duties in the galaxy.]

Are there other energies the Seraphim are working with outside of the Seraphim Blueprint energies?

Yes, they have other responsibilities. They have other agendas and other plans. They are not connected to this particular system. I come from an original group of thirteen.

Out of the thirteen Seraphim, why were you able to stay, or be spared?

I wasn't spared; I fought hard and won. The last time I had to do battle was about 200 years ago.

How can we assist planet Earth to avoid any of the problems that occurred in those times?

Start teaching these energies. It is very important for those of you who have that ability to teach the energies. The planet heals on a basis of one-on-one, on the basis of individuals healing themselves and other individuals. As we work to heal ourselves, we heal others. Teach the energies.

Break up the world's problems into smaller problems and handle what you can handle, rather than throwing up your hands because the job is too immense. Also, the energies work somewhat through bloodlines, so by working on yourself you are also working on your family members, indirectly without them having to know about it.

If these energies were strong and powerful in Atlantean times, then died out with that race, and are now starting to come back, are there any lessons that we can learn from those times to help us in their use now? Also have they come back in any other period of time?

After the Atlantean usage the Hebrews were the next group of people to use these energies. The Hebrews used these energies around 50 A.D. They were the creators of the Kabbalah, who had very strong connections to seven of the original thirteen Seraphim who were responsible for introducing the plan to our solar system. While the seraphic energies were widely available in Atlantis, the Hebrews limited their availability by shrouding them in secrecy. Around seven hundred individuals used the energies in Judea. The use of the Seraphim energies lasted about seventy-five years. It died out again because the individuals were too few to keep it going. It was, however, something that was very necessary at that time. It was an era when the Jews were forced to disperse from Palestine. Partly because of this dispersal [the *Diaspora*], fighting and warfare, and partly through the lack of interest of the younger generation, as well as the aging of adherents of these energies, their use died out. The times were suitable for great change and the seeding of the Seraphim energies, but were not suitable for the maintenance of the system.

The energies used by the early Jews and the Atlanteans were similar to each other, but quite different to what you're using now. In other words, by the introduction of Life-force Energy, or physical healing, we have a whole different take on the system. Rather than using the physical healing elements of the system, the Jews and the Atlanteans were using its spiritual evolutionary elements. Life-force Energy healing really begins with modern usage of the system.

Is there any reason why there is only one Seraph now, but there were seven Seraphim for the ancient Hebrews and thirteen for the Atlanteans?

Yes, there is a reason.

What is the reason?

I am reluctant to share this, but…

Is it something we should know?

Yes. {The Seraph starts talking directly through Ruth} *The other twelve angels were destroyed by dark forces, and I'm the only one left. That's why I don't want my name out there. I can't recruit any more angels to this program except angels of a different order.*

> The Seraph shocked us, for according to the Bible angels are immortal

[The Seraph shocked us, for according to the Bible angels are immortal. On other occasions the Seraph mentions working with other Seraphim, but what he means is that he is working with them in a general sense, not specifically with Seraphim Blueprint energies.]

Were you able to recruit Guardian angels?

No, but I can recruit the Thrones.

Is he currently recruiting them?

No

Is that because God isn't involved with this energy, or that he hasn't approved of the energy?

God simply is not involved with this energy. Here we have a problem with the definition of God. In any case, if you think of God as an entity separate from yourself then "God" is not involved. It depends on your concept of God.

How about the God within you?

The God Within knows about these energies, and this is not something that requires approval or disapproval.

Can we talk a bit more about the Seraphim that are remaining—other Seraphim besides this Seraph?

There are other Seraphim, yes.

Okay. So, there were only thirteen among all the Seraphim, who had these energies?

Yes. The Seraphim Blueprint was set up by thirteen Seraphim.

Does the number thirteen have any direct relation to the Disciples of Christ?

Not that I am aware of, but especially the Hebrews cherished the number thirteen in ancient times. The twelve disciples plus Christ does equal thirteen.

Does the number thirteen have any esoteric meaning?

Yes. It's a powerful number in numerology. Numerology is a local system—local to this planet. [Here Ruth interjects: "I don't know if there is any specific significance, but the Kabbalah traditionally has placed emphasis on the number thirteen. Jewish children were considered adults by their thirteenth birthday. My research has shown that to the ancients the number 13 was significant because there are 13 full moons in a solar year. There are thirteen waxing days leading to a full moon on the fourteenth, and then 13 waning days leading to a "dark moon" or New

Moon on the 14th. Also the Hebrew language uses letters as numbers, and it is considered significant that the Hebrew word for "love" אַהֲבָה *ahavah*, and the Hebrew word for "unity" אֶחָד *echad* both equal 13, and the two combined equal 26 which equals Yahweh, the Tetragrammaton, which biblical scholars consider to be the most holy name of God.]

After holding two channeling sessions with my students, at the end of 2002 I decided to sit down alone with the Seraph and ask about the order of angels known as Seraphim. When I began channeling the Seraph alone, I had my computer on nearby ready to write down anything that might occur in the session. While I was deeply in trance, suddenly the computer started making mouse-like noises that made me wonder if there was actually a mouse in the room. At the time I thought, "How cute that the Seraph may be doing that," but there was a little concern in the back of my mind. I ignored it. Two weeks later the sounds were no longer cute since they indicated a malfunctioning that caused my computer's hardboard and motherboard to crash on Christmas day… I almost lost the entire contents of this book. That the angel could wield such real power, whether intentional or not, was a new lesson for me.

The following information came through on the day I channeled the Seraph by myself:

"We were created as a group of eight thousand about 700,000 years ago, specifically to be custodians of this galaxy. Measured in your terms we are 25 feet tall, without wings and look like clouds of light. We have distinct personalities and distinct functions. Although we

appear immortal to humans, we can be extinguished through cosmic accidents and evil intent. We live in far-flung parts of the galaxy ministering to the needs of our flock. Our rewards come from working with other sentient beings that understand us, and partner with us when they can. I enjoy interacting with human beings, awakening them to celestial reality. I enjoy interacting with other angels, and other nonphys-ical beings. Our joys also come from completed projects involving mutual understanding and respect among the participants. We try to keep the galaxy running smoothly for the benefit of all.

Measured in your terms we are 25 feet tall, without wings and look like clouds of light.

Here on earth, there are seven Seraphim working with this planet, three working with the oceans and four with the continents. We spend all our time tinkering and tweaking multi-dimensional reality so accidents don't dis-rupt the delicate balance here.

At this time we are concerned about preventing a major war. This involves constantly neutralizing stress from the upper atmosphere through a cleansing process involving solar energies.

The analogy that is most suitable to all this is one of cap-tains and officers on an ocean liner. We are the officers of the ship called "Earth" which is moving through space at enormous speed. We watch out for any mishaps on board and try to eliminate obstacles in our way.

Those reading this, or any part of this book, who begin to feel bodily warmth, know that you are meant to do this work with us. The biblical accounts were correct when calling us "the fiery ones."

Another test is to place the cover of this book over your heart, and if you again feel warmth or some tingling sensation, you are meant to do this work. We need all the human help we can get.

The future is open for all to succeed in whatever endeavor they have chosen. We are here to make those pursuits more easily fulfilled. The complexity of the planet is welcomed as a natural flowering of seeds planted long ago. It is not to be feared, but accepted. In the next fifty years, you will be dealing with civilizations more complex than your own, and we are preparing you to meet them.

An era of tranquility is coming.

The positive note he ended on surprised me. The feeling that came through was one of certainty, and coming from his deep knowledge spanning hundreds of thousands of years was quite reassuring. Certainly keeping up with media events doesn't seem to project such Positivity, but as I write this, I am again reminded of the power of celestial reality, for the computer capitalized the word "positive" after I typed it normally, in a way that can only be unfathomable.

As I finished off the channeling session with the Seraph I returned the white stone crystal to its special holder on my nightstand for another day.

Stewart's Lesson

Stewart and I kept in touch over the years. Around the time I first moved to Sydney, he had left Japan for Hawaii and was living on the island of Maui just doing his thing. I believe that he and I both used Hawaii as a cultural decompression chamber when we were moving between America and Asia. By 2000 he had begun taking undergraduate courses at the University of Hawaii in Honolulu with the intention of entering medical school at the age of fifty-five.

One day I called him from California. "What caused you to want to start medical school at this late stage?"

"I need something more challenging than Rolfing. It feels too one-dimensional. I want to know what makes people tick."

"Is any medical school going to accept you?"

"I'm hoping to convince them that I will be useful in the area of medical policy, maybe as an administrator. Meanwhile I'm enjoying being a student again."

I could hardly suppress my skepticism. Stewart then changed the subject, "So, what are you up to these days?"

"Well you certainly had a big influence on me. You know

I will always think of you as one of my most important mentors."

"That's flattering."

"It's true. Remember how psychic I became through the pendulum you gave me? Remember when I called you one day to ask if *anyone* you knew used the pendulum to read the Akashic Records, and you said 'No,' you didn't know anyone who could do that. When I told you that I just discovered I could read the Records through using the pendulum, you encouraged me to charge $1,000 an hour for past-life readings. That got me thinking.

"Soon after that I connected deeply with the spirit of Yogananda's Babaji, who began training me. When I returned to America in '93 someone introduced me to a Seraph. You know—a very high angel. I didn't realize this special angel had been hanging out with me or giving me abilities that I never knew I had. Next thing I know the energy healer who made the introduction asked me to work with them to start a whole mystery school."

"Who are 'them'?"

"Oh, this energy healing teacher and the high angel."

"Okay."

"Well, we didn't actually start a mystery school, but we did study with the angel who downloaded amazing healing energies into our bodies. Of course, I didn't comprehend any of this at the time. I doubted that a Seraph had picked me to help spread these energies.

"Before this happened, with Babaji's influence, I had been working on a book about soul phenomena, but I was hesitant to publish it because it was and still is a bit scary. The implications for human behavior and understanding are enormous. Somehow I didn't feel ready to take on such an important project and be subjected to controversy and criticism. Therefore, when the Seraph made it clear that he really wanted to work with me, I chose to emphasize His work over my soul work."

"What is so special about these angelic energies? Are they really better than Reiki or other things out there?"

"Stewart, I don't know, but I have students who are also Reiki masters and they are telling me that these energies are quite powerful. Besides this system goes beyond healing."

"How does it do that?"

"Initially, I had no idea that there was an overall plan, or even that it was a 'system.' It seemed like the first stage of a doing a jigsaw puzzle. Looking back I can see the structure as a whole. It's simple and elegant."

"Elegant?"

"Yes, it's amazing. Because the first few attunements have to do with physical healing, l assumed that the whole system was just about healing."

"Wouldn't that be good enough?"

"Yes, if the system had just dealt with healing that would have been good enough, but it turns out that it simply was the basis of a more elaborate structure.

"Healing is an important basis, to be sure, because most of us live in our heads. Even as a doctor-to-be you probably take better care of your car than your body."

"You got that right."

"I remember hearing Ram Dass speak in California. You know the guy who wrote *Be Here Now*—the darling of the New Age movement."

"Yeah, I remember him and his colleague Timothy Leary, both high class drug pushers."

"That's him. Did you know that he supposedly became enlightened after meeting his guru in India?

"You mean the chubby blanket-wearing Neem Keroli Baba?"

"Yes, Stewart."

Then Stewart starts telling me something I already know from having read Alpert's book, but I let him tell the story again:

"When Alpert first approached his guru, Neem Keroli asked Alpert what kind of drug he had hidden in his backpack. Alpert sheepishly admitted he was carrying a huge stash of LSD. Then Neem Keroli asked to see it. When Alpert briefly showed him the tablets Neem Keroli grabbed them, and swallowed them all—maybe fifty tabs. Then the giggling guru continued talking as if nothing had happened."

"I guess you have read the same biography of Neem Keroli that I have. Anyway to bring you up to date about Ram Dass, when he was in his late sixties he had a major stroke that paralyzed his body and initially prevented him from speaking. I saw him earlier when he was still in his prime and an awesome speaker; then a few times after the stroke when he was only able to haltingly speak again. When I last saw him I asked him how the stroke had affected his enlightenment."

"What did he say?"

"He responded that previous to his stroke he never thought about his body. He was always seeking greater and greater mental highs. The stroke made him realize the importance of caring for the body.

"Therefore, I think the angels have got it right when they place such a strong emphasis on healing the body as a foundation for a major cosmology. When healthy, we can maintain a balanced perspective on our needs and can also be more generous and share our energy with others."

"Aw, Ruthie, come on—are you going to save the world?"

I giggled. "Yes, Stewart! Listen to how amazing the system is. A Seraphim healing uses only a few six-minute initiations to restore health. It takes four hours to receive the physical healing energies and another four hours to receive the emotional healing energies. Once installed, these intelligent energies repair whatever damage they can find in the body. Then the energies act like computer software fixing any errors. Most students immediately feel more together. In the first Level they also receive the ability to heal others with just one six-minute initiation."

"Can you give it to me now?"

"Sure. I'd love to. If you have a speakerphone, turn it on. I want you to have a hands-free experience, as it is quite relaxing; I am going to give you the first initiation, which is called Primary Life-force energy. Close your eyes."

When the transmission ended, I said, "Okay Stewart take time coming out." After a few minutes I asked him how he felt.

"I certainly noticed strong energy coming in through my crown chakra. Then it seemed to swirl around my body on a search and destroy mission."

"You're such a character. Yes, it does hit the main chakras.

That 'search and destroy' bit is part of its way of increasing pranic uptake in your body."

"So what comes after this?"

"After the physical healing energy, the angel gives out an emotional healing energy. Comparing the two, I know having the physical healing first seems odd because as the word *dis-ease* connotes, we have come to believe that bad emotions make us ill, and healing the emotional body first would seem more logical. I've concluded, however, that when the angels dazzle us with physical healing, they are intentionally being flashy in order to prove their existence, because most people don't even believe in them. When people feel powerful energy moving around in their bodies and notice immediate physical relief they are more likely to think, 'yeah, something is happening here'."

> When angels dazzle us with physical healing, they are intentionally being flashy in order to prove their existence...

"So where is all this heading?"

"I'll tell you some other time. Tonight I want you to take it easy, as the initiation you just received is really powerful, and you might begin to notice a boost in your energies by tomorrow. Do you remember the special personal stones that the School gave us?"

"Oh, yes, I still have mine somewhere."

"Well, they play a part in this too. Why don't you try to find yours again and maybe keep it on your body for an hour a day and see what happens."

"Too much trouble. Let's see how I feel tomorrow."

"Okay Stewart. Talk to you later. Bye."

The Stone Illuminated

It is seven-eighths of an inch long and three-quarters of an inch wide and pure white. If I can believe my psychic impressions regarding it, then it was quarried from a crystal mine in Poland and has spent 14,000 years in crystalline form. Its English School handlers energetically cleansed it for six days, and then likely programmed it with my photo, probably using a multi-colored, symbol that was part of the Arcadia School's paraphernalia containing elements representing a green chalice, a stylized white flower, the sun and the moon. Before beginning, the person performing the ritual probably aligned themselves through intention with cosmic forces as well as with the Earth.

All of this was done to make certain that they were attuned to the purest of energies when dealing with such subtle powerful forces. Those who programmed it enhanced its consciousness many times beyond what it already had as a simple white quartz crystal. Through their pure thought amplified by ritual, they gave it *purpose*. In sacredness they breathed intention into the stone, and with that it was given the title 'Opener'—opening its owner to cosmic and spiritual energies from everywhere.

Even before I received it, my Opener was already sending me signals, although I wasn't aware of that at the time. The signals it emits come from near and far, from across the room and across the galaxy. When it is not given a specific purpose it falls back into a general-purpose mode, which is all encompassing and all enhancing to its owner.

When my students receive their Openers, which I have ordered from various crystal mines, they naturally ask me about them. Although I don't discuss the ritual programming of the Openers with the students, I usually say that this one stone is likely to be the most precious item that they will own from that day forward. It will not only amplify the initiations they are about to receive, but it will calm them down when they are in a crisis. In the future it may even open them up to adventures beyond the currently known human repertoire—abilities such as time travel and teleportation. These abilities lie hidden in the hardware of our nervous systems waiting to be awakened.

The actual programming of each Opener involves a small ritual that appears to be a successful recreation of the Arcadian School's process. I now believe, however, that the new Openers' powers might go beyond what the School created, because the Seraph is fully involved in the process.

> These abilities lie hidden in the hardware of our nervous systems waiting to be awakened.

Just a few months ago my own Opener, which I have managed to keep safely for the past eighteen years, went missing. Normally I don't carry it about, but I was under a great deal of stress on that particular day, and had been wearing it on my body near where I live. For the next several days I didn't feel the need to hold it, and then when I wanted to use it for something and went to reach for it from its holder. It wasn't there.

Suddenly I remembered the last time I had used it, and thought 'Oh, no! I lost it on the street.' I started searching the neighborhood for anything white. I asked about it in stores that I had visited on that day. I did a complete house search, which ended up being a good cleansing. Then, when I failed to find it, I felt doubly saddened by the loss of something so sentimental, and also intrinsically part of my work with the angel, the Seraphim Blueprint and this book. I even had thoughts about the loss to future generations. When I am long gone, they might at least have a memento of how all this began.

My search went on for days. Although I am strongly psychic, when something is this emotionally charged it is difficult for me to look at it psychically. Also, I don't always consult with my Guides or angels, as sometimes I am just grounded in the experience, working within a more ordinary paradigm. After all, don't we all love drama sometimes? If the Guides and angels quickly and neatly resolved every difficulty, life might be boring.

Instead of consulting my Guides, I pulled out all the drawers of my dresser bureau. I cleaned my whole house. Nothing. Then about a week later I pulled my mattress away from the wall, and there it was. What a huge relief!

I vowed never again to wear it on my body outside the house. Although I can program a new one, I have not seen a stone quite like mine, and its milky sweet connections would be lost forever.

Stewart Follows Up

I was surprised when Stewart called back a few weeks after his initiation into the Seraphim energy and said, "I'm feeling really WHOLE! What a great augmentation of my physical well-being, I can feel energy flowing through every nook and cranny of my body."

"Come on Stewart. You must be putting me on."

"No, I truly felt something."

"Well, that's nice, but I really didn't expect to hear back from you."

"What can I say? I was impressed with the initiation. Would you like me to hang up now?"

"No, silly."

"Then what other goodies can you share with me?"

"Well, the special thing about the Seraph's system is that there is so little required. It's like taking some pills and forgetting about it. It can even replace meditation for many people. Nowadays who has time to meditate?"

"You can say that again."

"The Blueprint just takes a few hours every couple of months and that's it. Of course, in the meantime there is some adjustment to the energies, but most people find the adjustments rather pleasant. They get a bit high on the day of the initiations, and when that wears off they settle into a more elevated state of being. Even if an individual has no particular health problems, they still feel a sense of greater internal union. They see indications that their life is on track, and when I let them know about the next course they book in."

"Okay, I'm beginning to get the picture. But what happens after this healing?"

"You mean the next level?"

"Yes, where does it go from here?"

"Well, the next level is called "Seraphim Sacred Geometry." It is about breaking down karmic boundaries that limit us in this lifetime. Breaking through such restrictions allows for faster evolution."

"Do you mean some kind of karmic clearing process?"

"No. Prior to being born you negotiated with your Pre-birth Council on what tasks you wanted to accomplish in this lifetime. It is like going beyond this plan, and upgrading your cellular codes so that you can accomplish more than you previously thought possible. In your case, you are already breaking through these karmic boundaries by doing a medical degree in your fifties. It's about becoming more spiritually responsible."

"Yeah, I know about the pre-birth council—some wise guys sitting around a table. Prior to this lifetime I asked them if I could meet Marilyn Monroe. Guess what? One day I bumped into her in downtown Manhattan. Only problem was when I made my request I forgot to include a time factor. When I met Marilyn I was seven, and my mother was holding my hand as we crossed the street."

"*Very* funny," I said. "But the time factor is important and normally you are so street smart too. How did you get that wrong?"

Stewart continued, "Seriously, what can people expect to experience from the expansion of karmic boundaries?"

Prior to being born you negotiated with your Pre-birth Council on what tasks you wanted to accomplish in this lifetime.

"It's a bit hard to predict, but in my case I felt a tremendous development of consciousness when initiated into the energies at this level. And every year since I've noticed how my life plan is taking me into un-chartered territory."

"So where does the system go from there?"

"Well, Level three is called "Seraphim Manifestation," and it's about getting your personal and cosmic desires fulfilled. While these energies help us to achieve our personal desires, they also instill in us a desire to serve humanity."

"I don't know about serving humanity. Wasn't it Winston Churchill who said, 'Man will occasionally stumble over the truth, but he usually manages to pick himself up, walk over or around it, and carry on.'"

"Now, this is the Stewart I know! Seriously, though, don't you want to hear about Level four?"

"Okay, girl, tell me all about it."

"We call the next level—"Seraphim Cosmic Splendor." It deals with galactic forces and their interaction with our bodies. This level helps us to adjust to cosmic force fields that hurl our bodies through space at thousands of miles a second. According to the Seraph it turns out that our bodies are holographic pieces of the entire universe."

"As above, so below."

"Yes, that's the idea."

"Level four attempts to correct imbalances in our genetic makeup that no one on the planet has begun to think about yet. Most of us who have been brushed with Asian spiritual ideas assume that as Earthlings we evolved from past lives as plants or animals. But recently I have come to believe that a good proportion of us have extraterrestrial sources, both genetically and spiritually. I don't think you can read any of Zachariah Sitchin's works, starting with *The Twelfth Planet*, and ignore the evidence of E. T. manipulation of humans that started in ancient Sumer or even earlier. Otherwise how did the Sumerians change overnight from a primitive culture to one knowing about astronomy, writing, law codes, the wheel, and the city-state?

"All of the so-called 'gods,' whether mentioned by Sumerians, Greeks, Hebrews, or Egyptians, appear to have been selfish and self-serving. And yes, they had what seemed to us to be supernatural powers. But maybe they were really E. T.'s, and denied us some of these powers when they manipulated our gene pool. I believe more than half of our DNA has been purposely switched off.

"In other words we may be programmed to have extremely short lives compared to other civilizations in the galaxy. Having shortened lives would prevent us from achieving much in one lifetime and thus hold us back from cultural and technological advances that might threaten whoever manipulated our gene pool. The whole Adam and Eve story of being expelled from the Garden of Eden is probably a reference to the 'gods' limiting our abilities on purpose. The E. T.'s that created us didn't really care about us since we were their slaves to mine the gold on this planet to fix the depleted atmosphere on their own planet, and probably we were a throw-away model to boot."

"Oooh. So cynical."

"Stewart, these are not my ideas, but are from Sitchin's work and are confirmed by the Seraph. I can't seem to put them aside. If as evolutionary theory claims we evolved slowly on this planet then how come we are almost completely hairless when compared to other mammals, making us have to artificially deal with the severe cold climates that we have had here? *Again this must be due to E. T. manipulation of our genes.* If we have spent millions of years adapting to this place—through multiple ice ages—why don't we have a complete fur coat like other mammals? Also our lack of hair means we are more exposed to the Sun's harmful rays. Then, too, nobody discusses the stress of hurtling through space at 792,000 kilometers per hour. All these factors have to be stressful on the body.

"Maybe you want to join me in med school?"

"No, thanks. I think I will skip that in this incarnation. Stewart, the neat thing about working with the Seraph is that the system takes into account the defects in the human genome, correcting flaws in our make-up that helps us to survive and thrive better on this planet, since we are not perfectly adapted to it."

"Sounds good to me, but I don't have the time right now to hear any more. Meanwhile, thanks for what you gave me. Maybe next time you can top me up with some more energy."

"Sure." With that the call ended.

Just when I thought my understanding of the Seraphim system was almost set in stone, a few weeks later the Seraph surprised me with some new information.

The system takes into account the defects in the human genome, correcting flaws in our make-up that helps us to survive and thrive better on this planet...

The Tor

In early 2005 while I was daydreaming about my 1997 experiences in England, I suddenly realized that part of the Seraph's name was also the name for the famous hill in Glastonbury known as the "Tor." Although I had never heard the Seraph's name before, it did have an odd familiarity that I couldn't place. During my stay in Glastonbury, I had climbed the Tor, the small magical hill at the edge of town. I had found its symmetrical cone-shape covered with thick grass most pleasing to the eye. I had photographed it from several angles trying to get as much of the flat surrounding countryside into the picture as possible. At the Tor's peak were the remnants of an old church tower that simply capped the view.

Within days of making the connection, I asked the Angel about His name. When He said his name *did* refer to the Tor, I was dumbfounded. My thoughts tumbled over one another racing ahead to fathom the implications.

Considering that He had previously asked me to be silent about His name, I initially felt a bit dejected about this marvelous information since I felt I couldn't tell the full story here. I struggled to make sense of where this piece of the puzzle fit into the book if I had to be reticent about His name. It seemed like a huge burden to have to keep such wonderful news a secret.

Well, within a few days I was delighted, but puzzled, when the Seraph gave me permission to publish His name in this book. I am still adjusting to this surprising outcome, and have spent a lot of time considering the implications. Something must have shifted on the planet for this to happen.

Maybe the Good Guys are winning after all?

Thus I will continue with the story here of all that the Seraph has revealed to me, including His name. First, though, I need to digress a bit about *my* 'real' identity as I have been holding back a little until now.

Most of us 'know' that we are born with one soul. Well, in 1989 Babaji began gradually to indicate to me that about ten percent of the world's population has more than one soul at birth, or acquires another one, and sometimes more, additional souls some time after birth. At the time, I was completely flabbergasted about this idea, not having heard of it in any of my academic studies of world history or religions, modern or ancient. Babaji, however, insisted that multiple-souled people do indeed exist and that this is a natural phenomenon. Therefore, after much reflection and research, and noticing that the Encyclopedia Britannica has a heading called 'Multiple Souls,' I began seeing this phenomenon in many clients and came to realize that I was also born with two souls, and that both of my souls had been fused

Babaji insisted that multiple-souled people do indeed exist and that this is a natural phenomenon.

together for several lifetimes.

These two souls had some natural attachments to certain individuals I considered to be my soul mates in this lifetime, whom I met earlier in my life, including my mother. I believe that many of us have known either our mothers or our fathers in previous lifetimes. The whole discussion of multiple souls is part of another book I am writing concurrently, but it is of some tangential concern here.

About the time that I was exiting Australia and returning to the States in 1993, unbeknownst to me, my two souls became disillusioned with what was occurring in my life, and decided to arrange for their own departure from my body without 'telling' me. I didn't understand on a conscious level that anything major had taken place because my external life was changing radically as well, moving between continents as I was at the time.

Since nature abhors a vacuum, my previous two birth souls were immediately replaced by two new souls that had unique spiritual abilities beyond those of my former souls. I did notice the sudden enhancement of my powers in the area of spirit release and was most curious to know what was going on, not realizing there had been a soul change and I was now a "Walk-in"—a term introduced to the culture by Ruth Montgomery's book *Strangers Among Us*. She stipulated that when a soul wants to commit suicide but realizes how badly that will affect loved ones, it sometimes is sophisticated enough to arrange for stand-ins to replace it in the body.

Once back in America I did find it odd that I felt so emotionally detached from being there. On previously returning home, I had been glad to be in the States. After all, not long before, I had loved America enough to devote eleven years to my Ph. D. on American intellectual history.

After being in America a few years, though, I began to recognize that I had really changed on the soul level, and Babaji confirmed this. Then in 1997 I was traveling in England and had the unusual past-life flashback in the small town of Wells, near Glastonbury, that I mentioned earlier. This past-life experience was related to one of the new Walk-in souls that had joined me in 1993. Thus, when I asked the Seraph about my lifetime in Wells, He told me that He knew me at that time too. He knew the new soul that had entered my body and arranged for that visit to its ancestral home in England. *Thus, if I hadn't had the soul change I wouldn't be writing this book. It was all too unbelievable.*

The Seraph said that I shared some of the Seraphim energies with friends and family in that English lifetime too. Because the Church tended to brand such gifts as heretical, I was afraid to let it be known too widely that I was a healer. In that lifetime I was a simple peasant woman, and kept these things to myself.

I'm apparently more of a braggart this time round.

In the 1400s in England the Seraph had contacted me when I was twenty-one years old, a married woman with children, and I enjoyed his company and advice for about twenty years until I died in my forties. He was planting seeds that have sprouted in this lifetime.

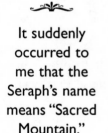

It suddenly occurred to me that the Seraph's name means "Sacred Mountain."

After recently reading Dan Brown's book *The Da Vinci Code*, and seeing its discussion about the Holy Grail and its code word *"Sang real"* which, in the context of that story, originally meant "royal blood" and slowly evolved to the words "Holy Grail," I began to see the connection between the Tor and the Seraph's name.

The first three letters of the Seraph's name are "SAN," which I thought of as the meaning "saint" as in San Francisco, which is Spanish for St. Francis. This "San" could also mean "holy" or "sacred." Then the middle syllable of His name is "TOR" a Welsh word for 'rocky hill.' It suddenly occurred to me that the Seraph's name means "Sacred Mountain." And that is exactly how He wrote His name for me across my field of vision in 1995—

SANTORIA

In caps just like that, but the letters were white against a dark background. I remember at that time I was confused because His name resembled a Spanish word 'Santeria', which is the official name for a fusion of West African religious practices with Spanish Catholicism that incubated in the Caribbean and is commonly known as Voodoo. When I asked my Spanish-speaking friends in California about the Seraph's name they said there was no such word in their language. I did find it odd that there seemed to be some other Latin-based connection, but over the years I simply forgot about it.

By the way, as an English speaker, it became natural for me to pronounce it as San-TOR-ri-a, with the emphasis on the second syllable.

The Seraph's Message

*P*ervasive peace is elusive in the universe because of the com-
*petition of all conscious life-forms to grow and thrive in a
relatively limited field of time and space, forms that all must
share as part of the third dimensional experience. Earth is on the
threshold of huge material and spiritual change that will allow
most humans to experience celestial reality directly. People will
start to use their five senses in an expanded way beyond the ordinary sensory perception they've been accustomed to. They will see
beings on the "other side"; they will hear the elementals of nature
talking to them. The trees, for instance, do have consciousness;
rocks and stones hold earth's memories, and rivers are aware.
Human beings will smell celestial perfumes that will waft
through the air from out of nowhere. The so-called "music of the
spheres" is real, and people will begin to hear celestial instruments that third dimensional instruments have tried to imitate
for thousands of years.*

*All of this will happen naturally as new souls are born into
human bodies that are better prepared for these experiences—
better prepared in both senses—the souls coming in will be more
evolved, and the bodies that house them will be better equipped.
There is no real need to do anything special to achieve such experiences. The teaching outlined in this book is for those who wish*

to speed up the process a bit. It's for those in a hurry. They will help to bring in the new experiences for everyone else—for the process is accelerated by collective participation.

There is no need to compare different healing methods. All healings are good. They are for the purpose of clearing and cleaning. Whatever feels most appropriate to the reader is fine, because who you really are is whole and holy underneath all that needs clearing or healing. There is no need to say this method is better than that method. Each individual naturally finds what best resonates with him or her and follows that.

As humans become more and more linked to one another globally, they will become more aware of the need for stewardship of the planet, which will help them to see this planet more from my perspective of overseeing this section of the galaxy. When all is said and done, humans are aspiring to put me out of a job! Just kidding. But it will be nice to have help rather than resistance when it comes to planetary issues.

Regarding many of your concerns about the treatment of animals on this planet, I want you to know that the animals live in an unbounded state. They are already at a place where humans are striving to be. There's no need to feel sorry for them or to worry about their existence as such. Their happiness, though, is entwined with yours, so be careful not to harm them or do needless experimentation with their ensouled bodies. Their existence is at a much higher plane. Their connection with unboundedness—the source of all energy —is not obscured as that of human beings often is. An animal's surrender to

The whales help form a "consciousness grid" across the planet that wouldn't exist if they weren't there.

Source is already perfect. As such they are guardians for you. The whales, for instance, help form a "consciousness grid" across the *planet that wouldn't exist if they weren't there. In other words, their high intelligence in the much larger area occupied by the oceans forms a type of relay station transmission, spaced at beneficial intervals, to keep an even pulsation of consciousness around the globe.*

As individuals who want to protect their lives, you can behave as responsibly as possible as an example to those around you. You can also interact with various governmental bodies as a first step to help animals and the environment of which they are a crucial part. Such activities mark the beginnings of a shift in consciousness. But a critical mass has to be reached in awareness or consciousness in order for changes to occur that will make a significant difference to help the earth, the forests, the trees and the animals. Large numbers of people need to be able to feel unbounded and to experience the natural world as a part of themselves. Then when a tree is cut down in the forest people will feel it and cry out in pain.

It's not as bleak a picture as it might seem because one person in an unbounded state can affect thousands, can affect millions. Because of your Internet connections and all your high technology now, that one person can have the effect to change many cultures. So a peaceful and ecologically viable planet is not an impossible dream, and its realization is becoming easier and easier as more and more people become aware. It is important for people to realize that true change takes place in consciousness first and then informs action. It is important for people who are awake to this to help others to reach that place too—and then to perform action from that state of awareness.

By giving out the Seraphim Blueprint, I am planting the seeds whose fruition will help to heal the rifts in human consciousness, which have come about because of the careless treatment of the body and also because of historical events that have long-term karmic implications for all involved. I like the line Ruth often quotes from Maharishi—"It's wise to prevent the birth of an enemy." By this she means the inability to really kill anyone, for the soul never dies, and as it is born into its next life-time it will harbor hatred for the same enemy from its previous lifetime and want to take revenge. Mowing down the enemy on a battlefield is similar to mowing the grass. It always grows back because the roots have not been removed. Violence is self-defeating. Since we are all literally one it's like having the right hand punch the left hand. In general, humans are simply pretending to be unique and different. Such a pretense takes an enormous amount of energy to maintain both individually and collectively.

As you evolve spiritually, celestial aspects of life become more apparent than earthly aspects. Stark black and white in most situations becomes more muted, more subject to nuances not noticed before. Yes, there will still be extremely polarizing events, but the wise among you will maintain their balance in such circumstances. For they know that this, too, will pass.

Embracing ultimate union is the goal, whose foretaste we can savor while the barriers holding the dimensions apart begin to crumble, just as when, at the end of the Cold War, the Berlin Wall came down. When we slowly become aware of the artificial barriers we have created between earthly and celestial reality, these constructs will self-destruct too. Some among you are already punching holes through that

It will become so natural to play in several dimensions at once.

wall. The Seraphim Blueprint is like a major 'crane' coming to knock down big chunks of the wall and carry them away.

Each of you who choose to participate in this program is doing your own individual part in dismantling the wall. There will come a time when everyone will look where the wall used to be and wonder what artificial force created it, because it will become so natural to play in several dimensions at once. That will be a time when we really hear the thoughts and wishes of Mother Earth and of the celestial spheres, as well as of the beings with whom we share this part of the galaxy. There will be many extraterrestrials that will be coming, and there are many here now. Some come from the light and some from the dark. More humans will be able to detect their presence and their agenda as time goes on. There will even be more technology that will make their presence known. Those of the ET's, whose motives are positive, can also help spread the positive effects of unboundedness and interactions with All that Is.

Rather than trying to explore the galaxy the way "the West was Won," we need to become comfortable with the idea of exploring the galaxy through fine-tuning our nervous systems to accept intergalactic communications of all sorts first, so that we follow the proper protocols in visiting such far off places later.

In addressing some of your fears for the future of this planet, I acknowledge that there will be earth changes taking place; some of them quite large; but still these are within the normal range. There is nothing extraordinary about the coming earth changes, even if there are those that do much damage, as all these changes are in alignment with the earth's cycles. In some years there are more, some years there are fewer. There are bigger cycles that take place, and then there are even bigger cycles that occur. Earth is going through one of the mid-range cycles now. There will be destruction for a while, but there will be a slowing down again of the rate at which changes occur. In another couple of thousand years there will be more cycles. There's no need to say this is "the end of the world" or this is extraordinarily different. The changes are just part of the normal cycles of the Earth.

Institutions will be changing. Governments will be changing. There is a new type of leadership coming into play. In the future there will be two types of leaders. One will be an antithesis of *the other. One type will seem more negative, more destructive; but balancing this out will be new super-paradigm people, who will be unbounded and able to lead from a state of semi-omniscience, like an avatar. There will be recognition of such leaders in a few years.*

It will seem as if evil will be taking over for a while; but in reality, this is all part of the plan, the plan to bring more harmony. It's the swing of the pendulum to go toward one side in order to feel the absence of the other side, so that absence will cause a vacuum that will be filled with more Positivity. (Note: the P was capitalized by spirit, as I typed it in lower-case.) Again this is just a cycle. It happened before; it will happen again. Now the pendulum is swinging more toward negativity. But again, it is all part of the plan. There is nothing extraordinary about this. A new wave of Positivity will be forming from this that will be much stronger, much more coherent and be able to be understood by many more people.

As I said, great international heroes are coming into play. They won't be allied with governments; they will be international heroes that will inspire people. Governments will start to lose their importance when real international leaders emerge.

One final word on this, please remember that for every man, woman and child now in a body there are 17,000 souls on the other side lending support to the rebirthing that the planet is currently experiencing. These trillions of interested parties are not going to allow this planet to be destroyed. They have a past, present and future stake in seeing a positive outcome to what many of you conceive as a fairly dire set of circumstances.

Love is the key, the doorway, to unboundedness. This is a very deep love that needs to be known—that is, it needs to be experienced directly and it is much deeper than what is normally portrayed as love, in the movies, and the media. Although similar to what people have experienced as love, this exalted Love is more like bathing in a pool of Love. Everybody has had this experience, either in the distant past or the distant future, which is all happening Now. Thus, the memory of that past/future experience serves to remind you that it does exist and is part of your potentiality to be recalled. This Love leads to unboundedness, or is unboundedness. The two are really the same. Love is Unboundedness.

I am blessing you personally as you read these words, for I have been with you throughout this entire experience. Know that you are blessed.

—Santoria

How to Connect
with the Seraph

Throughout history the angels that have connected with humanity most often have been from the two lowest choirs (orders) of angels—Angels and Archangels—as mentioned previously in Chapter 7—"What are Angels?" Therefore, when people think of angels, higher and lower, they usually think that the Archangels are the highest order because they have been the most powerful angels to influence us over the past three millennia.

Visionaries from Western cultures—notably those in the Bible—have occasionally reported contact with the Archangels Michael, Gabriel, Raphael and Uriel, making these the most popular angels of that order. The assumption has been that such a connection is the foremost that one could have. However, most visionaries who have reported communicating with angels found that they could not maintain a continuous connection with them. Human-angel conversations have traditionally been sporadic and undependable—now you see or hear them, now you don't.

Because of their close association with Source, any chance

communication with an angel by an individual gave that person exalted status in some circles. Thus, Emanuel Swedenborg, who regularly communicated with angels and who also was a respected scientist in his time (1688 – 1772), created the basis for a modern form of spirituality that generated a new religion—Swedenborgianism.

As I have written earlier, and as the Seraph has confirmed, if angels also wish to connect on their initiative with humans—and more and more of them do—it is possible to systematize the connection. Let me explain the basis for this statement. In my personal readings, I often see angels who have incarnated in human bodies. Such humans tend to be more gullible than most. They also are often late for personal appointments, and sometimes they are what can be characterized as a bit 'spacey.' The individuals themselves frequently recognize that they have these character traits. As I've previously noted, such lack of organization and focus is the exact problem of the angelic realm, and by incarnating in human bodies angels are trying to correct this defect. My point is that they often wish to make contact as they, too, are evolving, and their evolution requires them to become more grounded, more materialistic, and we serve to help them with this.

Therefore, in this day and age it is not unusual to connect with angels. You don't need to feel unusually special, although meeting them halfway is to be commended. By meeting them halfway, I mean promoting your spiritual side—allowing yourself to *enjoy* being pure and good. Furthermore, I encourage you to discern your highest and best motives in

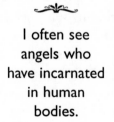

I often see angels who have incarnated in human bodies.

every situation that life presents. In this way you will

automatically be meeting them halfway.

Humans often tend to be fearful of delving into the spiritual realms because of potential darkness that might be lurking there. I will explore that issue in the next chapter. Here I want to give you a glimpse of the wonderful experiences you may enjoy when you connect with angels in general, and the Seraph Santoria in particular.

There are many ways to connect with angels depending upon how open any of the five sensory channels are in your body. Some people are visually oriented, some people are auditory—they hear things, and some people just sense things with their entire being. I happen to have the latter gift to a highly developed degree. However, because such things are rarely spoken of in our society, I didn't realize the importance of *feeling* things as a means of communicating with spirit until I was forty-five, as I have described in earlier chapters.

Getting Started

The best time of the day to initially work with angels is when you are first awakening or before going to sleep. At these points you are in a slight hypnagogic state, which is very suggestible. This means that before you start blocking the experience or before you realize clearly what is going on, the invisible beings can slip into your consciousness with their messages—or even actual signs. You may feel someone touch you but no one is there. You may hear a voice whispering your name; or you may see points of light around certain parts of the room. These signs may be vague or barely recognized at first—until they happen often enough for you to begin to recognize the pattern. This can indicate initial contact.

In my earliest two cases of contact with Spirit, first with Babaji and then with the Seraph, I initiated the contact by calling Babaji's name. When he came to me, I'm sure you recall that I didn't see anything, or hear anything, I only felt something. That was because only my feeling sense was open enough to have the experience. And in the case of the Seraph, he was introduced to me through another person— that highly clairvoyant teacher. Initially I didn't notice anything special about this angel. It was only when he gifted me with healing energies that I made a strong enough connection with him to begin recognizing when he was at my side. When he was around there came to be a noticeable difference to the way things looked in the room—everything became a bit brighter. Also I felt a bit high—exhilarated— but still focused enough to complete my chores or conduct a class.

In other words, once the introduction is made, no matter how that happens—whether you initiate it or somebody else introduces you to an angel, or you take a course in angelic energies—you can befriend the angel, especially when each of you has something to learn from the other. Perhaps a particular angel is thinking about incarnating as a human soon, and wants to learn as much as possible from you about the experience before he or she literally takes the 'leap of faith'— funny as that may sound.

As you may have realized from my experience with Babaji, calling the entity by name is important. The name of the Seraph—Santoria—is a wonderful way to connect with him. It is truly special that he is willing to share his name with humanity. Since he can be in hundreds of places at once, you needn't be concerned about calling him to your side. But remember that Santoria is one of the most exalted angels in the universe and should be treated reverently. You probably have several personal angels who can handle your parking needs. That is not Santoria's purpose in your life. He is here to restore humanity's balance and purpose in the order of things, and bring humanity back into alignment with Source.

Now I will provide you with another way to connect with the Seraph and with the system we call the Seraphim Blueprint, and it is through using the beautiful symbol that is on the next page. With Internet access you can download a color version of the symbol from the Seraphim Blueprint Website: *www.seraphimblueprint.com*. When you really need continuous support during some difficulty in your life I suggest that you place your palm down over the full surface of the symbol for up to eight minutes. If you are ill you may want to use the symbol as long as you like. While you are touching it, you will be connected to the angel much as a lamp is connected to a source of electricity—the energies will just continually flow into your body. These energies will flow wherever you might need them at the time because they are intelligent angelic energies.

You can also place someone else's photo face down on the symbol to have them experience the energies. However, I don't suggest you do this without their permission because they may feel the energies strongly and wonder what is happening to them. The Seraphim Blueprint energies are among the most powerful available on this planet, and one has to be careful to use them in an appropriate way.

Once you have noticed how much benefit you gain—how much you enjoy using the symbol to experience the Seraphim healing energies, you may feel ready to explore more information about the Seraphim Blueprint itself. This can be another powerful way to connect with this particular angelic source. The Blueprint process comes in six levels.

To connect with the Seraph touch the symbol with
your palm for up to 8 minutes

Here is an overview of the levels.

Seraphim Blueprint Levels

Level I—Seraphim Healing

This level heals us physically and emotionally, laying the foundation for spiritual growth. The first power of the system is for physical healing of oneself and others. The second power is also a healing power, but is emotionally based and called the Harmony Channel. Being initiated into these two energies allows for a sense of greater internal union and a stronger immune system.

Level II—Seraphim Sacred Geometry

This level is about breaking down karmic boundaries that limit our accomplishments in this lifetime. The key energies enhance rapid evolution. One is the supreme organizing power of the universe, and the other is the power to remove karmic limitations progressively.

Level III—Seraphim Manifestation

This level helps us to achieve our personal desires as well as our cosmic purpose more quickly. Receiving fulfillment on a personal level allows us to aspire to higher goals. The two key powers enhance intent, willpower and wish fulfillment.

Level IV—Seraphim Cosmic Splendor

This level helps us to adjust to the real cosmic forces that our bodies experience as our planet hurls through space at thousands of miles per second. Our individual bodies are holographic pieces of the entire universe. One energy repairs the damaged parts in our holographic etheric bodies, and the other helps us to adjust to an expanding universe.

Level V—Seraphim Planetary Healing

This level gives us tools to communicate with non-physical beings who can partner with us to help this planet in its many transitions. This power brings humanity into balance with the natural order. Specific initiations include harmonizing with elementals and vibratory beings.

Level VI—Seraphim Grace and Union

Once we have cleared out the heavier dross that we have accumulated over lifetimes, we begin to feel a real need to absorb beauty in our environment, and feel closer to Source.

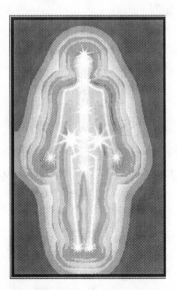

Seraphim Emotional Healing initiation

Protection

If we all had celestial vision we would normally see spiritual beings around others and ourselves. We would become familiar with the full range of ethereal beings and their impacts on human life, from those under whose presence we bloom to those under whose presence we wither. The former category includes angels, human spirit guides, and elementals **when honored**. The latter includes lost souls, demonic spirits, and elementals **when thwarted**. In order to understand how to protect ourselves from psychic attack from beings who are not in a body, first we need to understand the various categories of beings that exist on the other side.

As a psychic counselor, it is part of my practice to be aware of such beings. Although I lack celestial vision, I do have celestial sensitivity and touch, which means that I can pick up the vibratory signatures of these beings and identify their presence or absence around people.

In the auras of most people, I recognize the attendance of two or three angels. These angel contingents normally include a Solar Angel and one or two assistants. The Solar Angel is the being we ordinarily think of as our guardian angel, but whose "job" is to cultivate love, health, harmony, and happiness, and prevent bodily harm in emergencies.

Angels can go to great lengths to avert bodily harm. This was personally illustrated for me in 1995 when a desperate woman called me in California from Long Island, New York. I felt that she probably was down on her luck. The woman explained that in the morning she had contemplated suicide because her finances and situation seemed hopeless. I don't often hear such a cry for help. I became alert.

Then she proceeded to tell me that later that day, when she was walking down the street, a woman dressed all in white, with no overcoat, which was strange because it was a cold wintry day, approached her.

As they were about to pass each other, the woman in white said: "I know what you were thinking of doing this morning, and I suggest before you go ahead, you call this woman. She will give you a healing."

The caller continued, "Then she handed me a piece of paper with your name and phone number on it and turned to walk away. When I tried to see where she was going, a purple light blinded my eyes, and then the woman disappeared. I was so frightened that I ran all the way home. When I got home I found the paper still in my hand and that's why I'm calling you."

I gave her a healing then, but I was left wondering what had really happened. I had no advertisement in any paper in the rural town in New York where she lived. After consulting with several psychic friends, I concluded that what must have occurred is that the woman's own Solar Angel had taken human form in order to prevent her charge from acting out her thoughts. After that, I called her several times, and she seemed better.

As we can see from this example angels can be powerful agents for change in human behavior. While angels may act in a timely fashion during a crisis, normally we can't expect them to do so on a regular basis, for they do not have the same sense of time that we have. Rather than speaking the language of time and space, they speak the language of heart and soul.

Also on the helpful side of the equation are spirit guides, who are highly evolved deceased human beings, who, rather then being immediately reincarnated, choose to continue working with living people for a period of time. They are not assigned to work with a particular individual; it is more a matter of their preference and feelings. Unlike most angels, human spirit guides can be trusted with practical issues because they have lifetimes of experience behind them, and they remember it all. About one in seven people on the planet have spirit guide companion in addition to their angels.

All of these beings have a positive influence upon us when they are around. Although angels are commonly with us, the presence of the other spirits is more related to our life purpose. When I see a group of spirit guides around a new client, I will frequently ask the client if he or she works in the medical field. Almost invariably they answer, "Yes." One would think that doctors and nurses had enough of being overworked while they were in a body, but now I know they just can't seem to give up, even after they die!

The influence of the next class of beings, the elementals, is dependent upon human behavior. When treated with respect, they shower us with blessings; when mistreated, they attack us mercilessly. In the famous gardens of Findhorn the nature spirits and elementals happily helped raise fifty-pound cabbages in soil that was considered quite barren.

When elementals are in their proper devic form as caretakers of specific elements such as earth, fire, air and water, and are appreciated by humans, they reward us with the gifts of nature. When humans dislodge them from their elements and deny them their cosmic purpose, they can become angry and malevolent. When we build roads and buildings we are dislodging earth elementals. When we pave over creeks, we are displacing water elementals. They therefore pursue any human that crosses their path, and if that human's aura is weak, they take the opportunity to attach and cause real havoc.

When we build roads and buildings we are dislodging earth elementals. When we pave over creeks, we are displacing water elementals.

I am still researching the specific effects on my clients' behavior of the various elementals, but I have some clues. The earth elementals attachment will cause a person to remain stuck in old patterns. The fire elemental can cause a person to feel angry for no apparent reason. The air elemental may result in a person becoming ungrounded and unrealistic about their lives, while the water elemental usually precipitates emotionality and self-pity, and may also exasperate any pre-existing health problems.

The next class of beings is either inappropriate or harmful when attached to our auras or us. These include the second type of former human being, namely the lost soul, as well as demonic spirits.

Lost souls are deceased humans who don't realize that they have died, as in the movie *Ghost*. Part of the reason they fail to understand their own demise is that they can see and hear their living friends and relatives clearly, and they lacked simple knowledge concerning this ability before they died. They are also frequently traumatized by the death experience and too dazed to follow subtle cues they are receiving to go to the light. Many of these lost souls are children, whose understandings of the processes of soul evolution are incomplete. In addition there may be a rebellious attitude, even with knowledge of their own death. There may be a strong wish to stay here rather than do as they are told.

Furthermore, the adult lost souls, after wandering about a bit, may discover someone who shares their former earthly addictions, such as smoking or drinking, and because that living person's aura is weakened by these same addictions it is relatively easy for the lost soul to attach and vicariously enjoy the former habit through their host.

Then the living person has a lost soul attached and this condition can remain unchanged for years. It can also keep the host stuck in her/his bad habits and drain the host of his/her overall health and vitality. One of the signs of such ghostly attachment is severe neck and back pains due to a major auric opening in the back of the neck. Fears and concerns that the living host never had before may manifest because of thoughts actually belonging to the freeloader.

Of all the spirits, I am least familiar with the next class of beings—the demonic spirits. Although I rarely dealt with this energy in the first ten years of doing my spiritual work, lately I have been dealing with Dark energy in several formats. Normally we are given only slightly more than what we can handle, so I guess I have enough tools at my disposal now that my Guides must have concluded my nervous system is ready to deal with it all.

The first case I was given to handle was that of a very close friend, a psychiatric nurse in her early sixties, who in

1975 had trained with me to become a Transcendental Meditation instructor.

She met her current husband in a small self-development group in Texas that touted the loftiest aims for their members. The group leadership expected all members to make a substantial financial contribution in return for the security and warmth of the group. Nancy had been a member for five years, when finally something just didn't feel right, and she left the group with her new husband, whom she loved dearly.

About two years after she left the group, Nancy started having panic attacks for no apparent reason. Being part of a hospital community, her doctors thought it might be related to her mother's recent death. Nancy, however, felt she had been prepared for her elderly mother's departure. Nancy had a previous medical condition of osteoporosis, and her backbones were interacting with her increasingly frequent panic attacks in such a way, that she felt she was completely losing her health.

Since at the time I was still living in California, we only spoke occasionally over the six months or so that this took place. Then one day Nancy called me for a reading around the whole issue. I didn't have a clue as to what was going on, when suddenly she suggested that maybe it had something to do with the group that she had previously been a member of. As soon as she mentioned that, the hair on my arms stood up, and I knew we were on to something. Since I had only heard her say positive things about the group, I was surprised by this possibility.

I asked her for the names of all the top leaders. As soon as I wrote them down and checked their energy, I found three or four who had direct satanic connections. Touching their names, my own energy field began to drain immediately, and I had to be careful not to look too much at my writing on the piece of paper.

Next I asked Nancy for the names of everyone she still had contact with who was currently a member. I instructed her to cease all contact with these people immediately. I removed the psychic hooks from Nancy put there by the group leader and his wife, and I gave Nancy a Seraphim Healing initiation and healing immediately and several rituals to cleanse herself on a daily basis.

The first ritual is American Indian. I have my clients write a list of people they either feel some enmity towards, or have some kind of difficulty with, including their own parents. If it is a question of psychic attack, then the list needs to include everyone who is possibly suspect. Then I tell my clients to insert a name into the following sentence:

"I hereby remove any soul parts I may be holding onto of (name) for his/her and my highest spiritual good."

There needs to be a separate piece of paper with this sentence written on it for each person on the list. Then if there is also a photo of that person, it is to be used in the ritual. The person doing the clearing then says the sentence out loud with full intent and burns the photo and the piece of paper.

I then instructed Nancy to systematically go down the list of names, only doing one clearing per day. Once done, I told her to create a special protective shield around herself as follows:

Stand and imagine a wide ribbon of light circling around your feet in a counter-clockwise direction. Imagine that the ribbon of light slowly ascends to form a solid cone, leaving a narrow opening about a foot above your head, for spiritual energies to enter. Then imagine that the whole cone is covered with a Mylar (mirror-like) material whose reflection faces outwards. After all this is in place, say something like this: "I call upon the God Most High in the Universe to send back to its source any negativity directed at me."

New Agers who are always attempting to do the best for all concerned are likely to "improve" upon this by saying something like: "I call upon the God . . . .to send back to its source any negativity directed at me as Love." I am afraid, however, that this is not appropriate when dealing with the Dark Side.

In terms of lifestyle changes to protect you from negativity both in the physical and non-physical realms, here is my list of suggestions:

Do:

✦ Associate with positive-thinking people who lead clean lives.

✦ Meditate to clear out stress from your own body and mind, which will also enable you to eventually attract angels and guides who enjoy being around individuals who are vibrationally attuned to them.

✦ Imagine yourself playing with white light whenever you have a free moment, like waiting for a bus or standing in line at the bank. You can visualize yourself swallowing a glass of white light in liquid form; you can bathe in white light as you shower in the morning. You can swirl a Hula Hoop of white light around you and bring it up over your head, enclosing you like an inverted ice cream cone.

✦ If you have a continuing headache, or neck pain with no known cause, you may want to check with a good psychic to determine whether you have some negative entity around you.

✦ Directly invoke the presence of angels or spirit guides

through prayer. You can pray to the well-known angels, such as Michael or Raphael, and now that you know about Santoria, you can call upon him in extraordinary situations.

Don't:

ᴥ Remain close to a friend or lover whose energy is draining you. It may, however, not be the friend, but the entity in the friend's aura. A good spiritual counselor can often clear the aura of your friend without their having to be aware of this process. (We don't have to ask permission to correct cosmic irregularities.) Again, such a clearing may be temporary unless that friend or lover takes steps to strengthen their own auras.

ᴥ Have your body parts pierced. Although body piercing is fashionable, it is a subtle invitation to such spirits because not only are you weakening the body's meridians, but also the rings that are inserted signify a willingness to be "chained."

ᴥ Visit bars, hospitals, and prisons. Famous former prisons, which have become major tourist attractions, like Alcatraz in San Francisco Bay, are a serious hazard. The scenery may be beautiful and the history intriguing, but a negative entity attachment is a possible souvenir.

ᴥ Consume alcohol, tobacco, and other recreational drugs. All these substances have had historical ritual associations. When used in their proper ritual settings, where the elders knew how to protect the whole group, they were relatively safe. In the last one hundred years we have altered their usage in several significant ways. These sacred substances have been introduced to the general population stripped of their ritual context. Instead they are enjoyed socially, and due to their wide availability at a single gathering two or more of the substances may be taken together.

Following most of these recommendations will both help you attract angels and guides and repel lost souls and elementals, but there are always some exceptional circumstances that are difficult to explain. In fact a client came to me a few years ago wondering why his outstanding medical inventions were so little appreciated. He said that he had developed a cure for many forms of cancer. Even at that time I was politically aware enough to know that the medical/pharmaceutical industries might not appreciate a real cure for cancer, as it would greatly diminish their profits. Placing that thought aside though, I psychically searched his particular situation to determine what the problem was. I discovered that he had lost his complete set of angels ten years earlier. Frequently a person will lose angels due to substance abuse, but in his case my Guides told me it was because of his flying in a plane—a case of going too fast for your angels, I thought. After asking him about his flying experience ten years prior, the real scenario was more bizarre. He was a daredevil skydiver who made over a hundred jumps that year. Note the word "daredevil." In essence he was adding danger upon danger, and not respecting the human vessel, so the angels said "we're out of here."

Testimonials

Over the past decade, as the Seraph dispensed his beautiful energies, people have spontaneously wished to share some of their amazing experiences. In this chapter I will present a sampling of the letters and comments of people who have experienced either a healing from the Seraph through me or through one of the workshops. Many of the students have had no previous experience with healing modalities, and these students are the most euphoric in their descriptions of the results they have experienced.

Eleanor learned Seraphim Healing from her daughter, who was enthusiastically teaching the Seraphim energies in a small northern Queensland town. Eleanor is a midwife at the local hospital in that area.

As a midwife, I worked on some babies whose mothers had drug addictions. I found that the Seraphim physical healing energy was too strong as the babies squirmed a bit when I used it, but the Seraphim harmony energy was good. So when I used this energy on the little one that hadn't slept for three days, he slept for an hour and a half. He had his first really relaxed sleep where his hands weren't clenched. The nursing staff noticed and asked what I was doing, and the next night they asked me to help out again. They come and get me to settle babies. Even people who are heavy smokers have babies who go through nicotine withdrawal symptoms and have difficulty settling as well. Another nurse at the hospital has already done Level 1—Seraphim Healing.

—Eleanor, Queensland

Here is a testimonial from Alex, who had only just completed a Seraphim healing course in San Francisco when he suffered a serious arm injury resulting from a bad fall. In the class he had learned how to invoke the Seraphim healing energies. What follows is his e-mail to the rest of the participants in his Seraphim Blueprint class:

Hello Dear Seraphim Angel Energy Friends, Happy New Year to all! Unfortunately, my new year did not start all that well. I fell so badly last week that I hurt my left elbow severely. It was dislocated and is also broken. My instant reaction was to support it with my other hand and I had the intention of mixing the two Seraphim healing energies in order to get some immediate relief. It was an excruciating pain, but somehow I managed to stay calm. After the x-rays were taken in the emergency room I met the doctor. She was in total disbelief that I would be the person whose x-ray she was holding in her hand. She said that she would expect me to scream in pain and to cry and to beg for painkillers. Instead, I was walking up and down the hallway totally calm. She verified my identity twice to make sure I was the right guy. I told her that I am ok with the pain and that I would prefer not to get any pain medication. But of course, she didn't believe that was possible to set the joint back in without medication, so in the end the doctors and nurses collectively talked me into administering morphine. I still have shattered bones in my elbow now for the 8th day and have only taken two painkillers in this period. The doctors advised me to take pills continuously every 2 to 4 hours. They said that otherwise the pain will get totally out of control and it will beyond the point where it is possible to get rid of the pain using any medication. I do attribute my really high pain tolerance to the use of the energies. And I wanted to share this with you. I finally have my operation scheduled for tomorrow (Friday) morning at 8:45 for about three hours. The prospects laid out before me are not satisfactory at all. It ranges from a pretty high risk of having a permanently stiff arm to the best-case scenario of regaining some limited use of the elbow. The doctors told me that it could not be expected after an injury like that, that I would regain the full range of motion. But I am just not prepared to accept that ruling. But based on the doctors' diagnosis it would take a miracle to get my elbow working again properly. But that is ok. Miracles happen all the time, right? I would very much appreciate if you could you please send me your mental support. My best wishes and greetings,

—Alex

Jana is a young, bubbly Australian immigrant from Serbia who attended several levels of the Seraphim work and she had the following story to tell the group in one of the sessions:

> Before Christmas my girlfriend was very worried because she was having her in-laws over for Christmas Eve dinner, and she knew how uncomfortable she felt around them because she always felt judged and not accepted. So the day before they came, I installed a Seraphim energy grid in her home. And, lo and behold, when they came over they were so kind and completely different than before. My friend was amazed and thought it was extraordinary.

—Jana, Sydney, Australia

Dzintra, the proud mother of two beautiful girls in their twenties, is the teacher of the Seraphim Blueprint who is responsible for goading me into writing this book. With her strong clairvoyance, she was one of the first people to sign up for all the Seraphim healing work I made available in Sydney when I first arrived back in Australia in the late nineties. Here in her own words are her initial reasons of why she was impressed with the healing:

> A couple of weeks after the course I had a really bad headache and an upper respiratory tract infection. I was coughing. I was really sick, but it hadn't gotten to the chest. And I knew that if I didn't do something about it, it would become bronchitis. So I thought I will give this Seraphim energy a try. So I had both my hands covering my throat and did the healing. Then I fell asleep. The next morning when I awoke I couldn't speak. It seemed really, really bad. Then the following day I woke up and it was clear. I had taken no antibiotics. It just stopped. I hadn't been to the doctor. So what I think Seraphim healing does, whatever your illness is, is to concentrate it. You might first have a healing crisis where it gets worse, and then it's gone. That was the first time I used the energy.
>
> —*Dzintra*

For those of us trying to lose weight, the following story is rather amazing. I have yet to meet Cheryl, as she was taught by one of the student teachers of the Seraphim Blueprint.

> After completing Level 2, I had the most unexpected thing happen. I have always tried losing weight, but the kilos never stayed off. After I took Level 2 though, with absolutely no intention to lose weight I started to drop a kilo a week. That has been going on for eight weeks now! I feel it has something to do with the sacred geometric changes that we use daily with these new energies.
>
> —*Cheryl, Sydney*

I received the next e-mail from a woman in America who battled depression most of her life. She had had a short telephone consultation with me, in which I combined the Seraphic energies with other treatments that Spirit Guides have taught me over the years.

Dear Ruth,

My life has been a nightmare for so many years, that I am in awe that it has changed so quickly. This is what I e-mailed to my friend Diane this morning: "The tendency to depression is gone and that is such an incredible relief. Now, when negative thoughts come to mind, instead of spiraling down into the slough of despondency, they just melt away in mere moments all by themselves. I am still amazed."

I have been to so many people who were unable to help me, who wanted to prescribe drugs and send me on my way, who had no understanding of what I was going through. I have had to deal with a lot of anger toward all of them the last few days. I kept telling myself that they just didn't know, but all the harm they caused in their ignorance! I don't know if you are familiar with Ernest Holmes books, but it was helpful to for me to "re-identify" these people as being One with God.

I have, for years, wanted to get to the point where I, because of my empathy with people suffering from depression, could help others who experienced what I have. So, I would like to learn to do what you did for me.

I have so many questions...!

Carol

Again, the following testimonial is a letter to me from a student of one of the Australian Seraphim Blueprint teachers. This is the story that made the biggest impression of the power of the Seraphim energy grid that the Seraph has bestowed upon us.

My husband left work after approximately 25 years at the railways, a job he has had since high school. Although it was his choice to leave, having taken a voluntary redundancy, he was still very anxious and scared leaving his 'comfort zone' to work from home, especially given that he was 51 years old, with four boys still at home. Not to mention we were going through a difficult time in our marriage and neither one of us was balanced at the time. However, we held a Seraphim healing workshop at our house and placed a Seraphim protection grid around most of our home, including Greg's new 'office,' which had previously been our dining room. The office also happens to be a part of our lounge-room (L-shaped) where our four boys constantly watched TV, etc. In other words, it was the busiest part of our house but it was all we had with no other room to spare.

He left work in January. 2003 and immediately after the workshop in February, the phone started ringing continuously. He had offers to work in Sydney, Perth, England and Europe. He was totally overwhelmed and stunned. Big companies rang up with offers. He didn't accept any, because the reason he left work was to spend more time at home.

Instead he accepted an offer to work with a private consultant. He is still doing contract work and has work into the foreseeable future. It has been a big learning curve for both of us and occasionally he still gets phone calls for job offers, but he is happiest working from home for now. As soon as I get my diploma in therapeutic massage, I hope to work away from home a few days a week and, hopefully, I too will get lots of offers! Thank you for bringing the Seraphim healing to Australia.

—Diane, Sutherland, New South Wales

Muriel is a senior, who for whatever reason decided to take the Seraphim Healing workshop about five years ago. Her real passion is music, and when I was taping her for this testimonial she just gushed on and on about all the sudden good luck that seemed to follow from her putting a

Seraphim healing energy grid into her home.

My son and daughter-in-law share the house with me in Ashfield. My son had been in a business partnership from 1985. The partnership had worked well for the first ten years, but in the last five to six years things hadn't been going well. The partners, husband and wife, had not been sharing their full responsibilities and left more and more of the running of the business to my son. My son was beginning to feel pressured by the amount of work he had to cover, and it was unpleasant to be in a partnership that you really want to be free of.

He had been approaching his partners for a number of years about the possibility of winding up the business. He tried to point out to them that it wasn't making a sufficiently good return, and also that he was taking on too much responsibility. Why not wind up the business while there was still some capital available to them as their share of the assets of the company? At first they were reluctant to agree to his proposal and he continued to work with them, but it was beginning to affect his health.

On the Friday evening when I came home from the city, a few days after I put in the Seraphim healing grid into our home, my daughter-in-law was at the front gate waiting for me. She was saying "Quickly, quickly Mum, come quickly. You don't have to cook dinner for us tonight. We are all going out. Ross wants to go out and celebrate the closure of the company."

I said, "You don't mean that that company has been wound up?" She said: "Yes, this morning the news was given to Ross that the partners were happy to fit in with his suggestions."

They hadn't lost everything. They all received a good sum of money. Furthermore, they all parted very good friends. There was no hostility at all. It was wonderful. I really thank Ruth for the help she gave us with the attunements to open up the Seraphim healing to us. I can't tell you how grateful we are for that wonderful result.

—*Muriel, Ashfield*

Here is another gem from Eleanor, the Queensland midwife:

A friend of mine has a gray mare named Mazurka that had a fight with another horse through a fence and had a gash on its hind leg. I decided to send Seraphim life-force energy distantly to the horse. The next day, when I went up to the fence, the horse came up to me and wanted me to heal its hind leg. It came right up to the fence and whinnied at me, so I went over and did it. It was interesting to know that the distant healing did work, and then twice the horse came over and let me work directly on him. It did heal faster than we were expecting.

When Naomi first heard me speak at the 2000 Sydney Mind Body Spirit Festival, she immediately decided to do every course that I was giving during my stay in Sydney that year. She was highly stressed and searching for something that could make sense out of the different spiritual modalities she had previously studied. With each course she took with me, her stress levels decreased and she later said the Seraphim Blueprint system was so simple that she finally stopped looking for alternatives. The following testimonial is fairly recent and reflects her increasing expectation that the Seraphim energies can be used to heal her elderly father, whom she loves dearly.

Dad is well after the hip operation, which went brilliantly. The doctors were amazed how quickly the scar healed without infection and how quickly he was getting around again, due, no doubt, to his strength of spirit, but also to our prayers, our nursing and the Seraphim energy. My father complained the first day home that his leg was tired and asked if I would massage it. I thought this was a good chance to improve his circulation as well as give him the energy (though I didn't tell him exactly what I was doing). I nearly started laughing when he told me "I had healing hands," and he wanted me to massage the leg every day after the first day. He was out of hospital in a week, and my sister and I stayed with him for that week and three weeks at home until he recovered.

—*Naomi, Sydney*

In another e-mail from a young American client, who suffered from depression most of her adult life, we see more evidence of a miraculous angelic healing.

Ruth,

Whatever you and your powerful angels did for me last Thursday, it has had a dramatic (revolutionary!) effect. It's wonderful, and I sense that I am only beginning to experience the changes. I don't know how to describe what's been happening. So many of my negative feelings about myself have simply VANISHED. I've struggled for so long with feelings of low self-esteem, shame, embarrassment, and social awkwardness, and suddenly I seem to have achieved a complete transformation. I feel confident in the presence of others; I have so much more energy and focus; and I am finally able to do many of the good things for myself that I have been meaning and trying to do for so long.

Many of my problems over the years have centered on my sexuality. I've had terrible difficulty feeling attractive. Even though I have been told many, many times that I am beautiful and desirable, and have had many men who've expressed their interest in me, I haven't been able to FEEL attractive, or believe that I am deserving of a man's attention. After my session with you, all this has changed. I have gone from feeling rather desperate and unworthy, to KNOWING that I have what it takes to attract a man, and to create a healthy, enduring sexual relationship. I finally feel like I am in full possession of my body!

Thank you so much, Ruth, and thanks to whoever or whatever guided me to you. I'm looking forward to our next session.

—*Rachel*

Seraphim Healing and Cancer

I began to seriously consider treating cancer with Seraphim energies when my very close girlfriend, Setsuko Ichige was battling cancer for her life. This is a statement she made to fellow students in a small Tokyo Seraphim Healing Teacher Training course a few years ago:

> The fact that I am attending this workshop today to become a teacher of Seraphim healing is a miracle in itself. Nine years ago I was diagnosed with breast cancer and had to have a mastectomy. The cancer had already spread to my lymph glands and I was left with lymphoma. The best cancer centre in Japan treated me until a year ago when my doctor showed me a chart indicating that my body was riddled with cancer. He said we have tried every form of chemotherapy on you and nothing is working. He gave me a letter of introduction to a nearby hospice, basically giving me permission to die. If I hadn't started using the angelic energies, I probably wouldn't be talking with you now. The cancer appears to be on hold.

> —*Setsuko Ichige, Tokyo [Translated from Japanese]*

Although many people report that Seraphim healing is a powerful healing tool, the angel has cautioned us to use it against cancer only in carefully selected instances. Since this was his first instruction on the subject, I often avoided using it with cancer. Without proper research, we cannot claim that a spiritual energy can cure cancer.

The allopathic medical profession believes that cancer begins when a misguided cell duplicates itself over and over again. Since the cancer itself is a living being and Seraphim energies add pranic (Sanskrit term for "life-force energy") energy to the body, or to the cells, the use of Seraphic energy immediately over the cancer site might actually promote its growth. That's why we have to be extremely careful about using Seraphim life-force energy to attempt to treat cancer.

The Seraphim harmony energy is less risky in that sense.

Because Seraphim healing boosts the immune system, if the person had cancer of the throat, for instance, it is recommended to keep the healing away from the throat. Instead, go to the kidneys and to the solar plexus and work from those areas to boost the immune system.

Many people who have exhausted the resources of the medical profession turn to alternative therapies. The Seraphim energies might help on an individual basis, but we don't want to raise expectations too high. Most of us are not trained as allopathic physicians, and we might not have a clear picture of what is really happening in this complex arena.

There can be a million different reasons why a person has cancer. Even an enlightened sage like Maharishi Mahesh Yogi would often say that the ways of karma are unfathomable. In some cases a person has cancer because they are looking for a socially acceptable way to suicide. They really, truly on a soul level want to die, and if they want to die then trying to cure them is interfering with that process. So there are so many different scenarios with something as powerful as cancer. If you ask on a soul level why the person is suicidal but not on a personality level, the answer might be the difference between social norms and private desires. For example in a bad marriage where the wife really wants to separate, but nobody in her family supports her getting a divorce, then she unconsciously allows cancer to form in her body as an easy way of leaving the marriage through death.

Besides the frequent example of spouses trying to end a marriage through cancer, there are probably an equal number of cases in which the person is being alerted in a roundabout way that they are actually healers and need to be healing others in order to heal themselves. Since many people do not think of themselves as healers when they are young and don't choose to study medicine, they spend their lives working in jobs that have little to do with their soul's purpose of healing. Therefore the universe gives them cancer so they have to focus on many different healing modalities, and some of these individuals begin to recognize that they are actually strong healers and begin to work on others, thereby recovering from cancer themselves.

Recently we have cautiously begun to use the Seraphim energies when approached by people with cancer, and we have had some success. The energies are known to boost the immune system, which will greatly help fight any disease or malfunctioning in the body. It may also help greatly to have the person know that they are using spiritual and angelic energies to heal.

The Seraph Answers More Questions

How does the Seraphim Blueprint compare to other types of energy healing?

There are many flavors of ice cream. You each have your own favorites. Similarly there are many healing vibrations in the universe. What is important is what appeals to you, what excites you now. It may not be the same energy that you will need five years from now. The many different healing modalities all have a contribution to make, because your nervous systems are so diverse—in experience, in history, in soul-dimensional level, in accomplishment—whether you need more physical healing, more emotional healing. It varies.

Is it okay to mix different healing modalities?

Certain of the Seraphim energies can readily mix with other energies. How well they can mix really depends on the energy you are working with. This particular system mixes well with other energies, but it doesn't mix one hundred percent with everything.

Is it important to receive all of the Seraphim energies to achieve a level of completeness within us, or is it enough to receive just a few of the energies?

It's case by case. Some people will feel very complete just doing some of the Seraphim Blueprint work. Others will feel the need to do different practises in addition. This system is like icing on a cake to bring you to enlightenment.

Isn't it too difficult to acquire healing abilities as an adult if you were not born with such gifts?

In general, people have the misconception that such healing powers are God-given gifts from birth. What is not realized is that the human body is like a huge mansion with many secret rooms that have been closed off and left unused for a long time. With the help of angels and guides, these secret rooms can be opened, cleansed, refurbished and used.

What kind of healing can you give a person who is on drugs?

Drugs generally open up the aura of a person, allowing entities to attach more easily. Even prescription drugs weaken the aura. You can use Seraphim healing energies on them; however, in the same way you use it on anyone else.

Can the Seraphim Blueprint energies be contaminated?

No, they cannot be contaminated. They can't be taken over by negativity. They can only be used as they were initially created. There have been students in our classes who said they weren't feeling the energy. Although, sometimes "not feeling the energy," means simply not sensitive to energy. Sometimes "not feeling the energy," means literally that they're not getting the transmission. The reasons they are not getting the transmission often has to do with personal karma or some kind of unconscious resistance.

Note on the Seraphim Energy Grid

The Seraphim grid is a protective healing device. When you take the first level of the Seraphim Blueprint, you will be able to install such an energy grid in your home, or your office, temporarily, conditionally or permanently. Previous students have placed such grids in hospitals, child-care centers, and political assembly halls. Although the grids were not initially intended for open space, some students have experimented with putting them over their vegetable garden plots and have found them to work quite well.

Do all the Seraphim Blueprint Openers form a grid of light around the world?

The answer is yes; they do form a grid of light around the world. They magnify a person's consciousness when they're held, and if a group of people is holding them, they almost double the energies. So it's about one and a half times stronger with everyone holding their Openers than if they weren't holding the Openers at all. They do connect the individual more with celestial beings and with universal energies. The Openers can enhance healing power. They are an example of intelligence contained in a rock. Think of them as being like antennas.

NOTE: Seraphim Healing has been reported as being helpful in the treatment of the following:

- ✦ Arthritis
- ✦ Headaches
- ✦ Carpal tunnel syndrome
- ✦ Alcohol/tobacco addictions
- ✦ Colds/flu
- ✦ Broken bones
- ✦ Chronic fatigue syndrome
- ✦ Stress
- ✦ Immune disorders

The Seraph's Abilities

The issues broached by my students in the following questions illustrate their desire to dialogue with the celestial beings that are responsible for keeping our part of the universe sane and orderly. The students cautiously explore human limitations in working with angels and look forward hopefully to a time when communication between humans and angels will be easier.

Can you be in more places than one at any given time?

Yes, I can be in thousands of places at one time.

How many people can you simultaneously initiate into the Seraphim Blueprint energies?

I can dispense the energies to millions of people at a time, as in a radio transmission, for instance.

Planetary Issues

Ruth's Opening Remarks: As we progress through the Seraphim Blueprint levels and achieve personal physical, mental and emotional healing, we bring ourselves more into balance. When we bring ourselves into balance, the planet also benefits. When we raise our own vibration, we also raise the planetary vibration.

For those who have been exposed to the dire predictions based upon the end of a major Mayan Calendar cycle in the year 2012, the angel's response seems more logical and less apocalyptic. According to the Seraph the year 2014 is significant, and the Earth may become unbalanced then. Lack of water is a very serious problem. I have sometimes asked the seraph about global warming and nuclear disaster, but the angel seems more concerned with the future lack of water and overpopulation. He predicts that in 2014 the water shortage will be extreme. Water will be critically short in Australia in 20 years time; in North America, Europe and China the crisis will hit in ten years' time. Africa has a problem right now. More needs to be done about this issue.

He feels that the best approach for us to assist the planet is for those of us who are already teachers of the Seraphim Blueprint to begin teaching these energies. The planet heals on the basis of individuals healing themselves. As we work to heal ourselves, we heal others. The Seraph suggests that we break up the problems into small problems and handle what we can, rather than throwing up our hands because the job is immense. The energies work through bloodlines, so by working on ourselves we are also working indirectly on our family members. While there is no specific research to prove this, we have some inkling of this through anecdotal evidence. What the mechanism might be is unknown.

How can we heal the planet without having to go through the whole political process? Can we do it through meditation or collectively help it along somehow? Do we have to first heal ourselves as human beings, prior to working on the planet?

No, you can heal the planet at the same time as you are working on yourself. There are planetary healing energies associated with the upper levels of the Seraphim Blueprint. But if you want to do something right away, The Harmony energy from Level 1 is useful in doing planetary healing.

Try this visualization exercise and see how it feels. First imagine the planet the size of a soccer ball sitting in front of you in mid-air, and you put both hands around the planet. Holding it, you can send the healing to the planet as a whole. Visualise the energy going to where it's needed. You can do that for about six minutes and that will be enough at one time. Do this whenever you feel like it. So when sitting in the car or a waiting room, you can just do it. Yes. It's a good exercise.

> Imagine the planet the size of a soccer ball…and you put both hands around the planet. Holding it, you can send the healing to the planet as a whole.

Any healing work assists you as well. This whole system, especially, seems to rejuvenate oneself as well as the person who is on the receiving end of the energies. The energy channel opens to you as well as to the person receiving the healing. You both get healed.

Can married couples heal the planet in some unique way?

Yes, you are in union—so it definitely helps the situation (for example: releasing stress from the marriage). It is important to understand that when an individual uses these energies, they work through bloodlines and through relationships in union. Therefore, as you work on yourself and others, you are also transmitting some of this energy through people related to your union by blood and other social relationships.

Electronic Smog

It's apparent to me that the planetary mass culture places too much emphasis on the needs of the lower three chakras, and any sacredness they might have has been lost by this bizarre focus. I want to know, were things meant to be this way, or are we retarded? Is something going to shift this energy so that the higher chakras can be more involved at a societal level?

Good question. .... I want to say we do see noise at all levels. There are many noisy things on this planet. By noise I mean electrical frequencies that are really unnecessary, incompatible with human beings. I'm referring to microwave ovens, microwave energies, high radio frequencies—all the electronic equipment around. Some of you are not allergic to these energies; but some of you are. It's important to reduce this electronic smog. This is a contributing factor to confusion on the planet. Very few people are aware of it because it does not serve industrial needs or bottom line profits to eliminate this kind of smog. There has to be a bigger movement to replace this technology with technology that's more compatible with human beings.

To answer your question more directly, one of the benefits of population explosion is that it enhances the cross-communication of all minds in the global village, even without television or the Internet. In fact, if you all turned off that equipment, your telepathic powers would become much stronger. Thus, over time, the upper chakras will become stronger in the general culture as more of you seek that enhancement.

Just become responsible for your part of the solution.

Are there technological advances happening now to bring about more compatibility between humans and machines?

Such discoveries that circumvent the current situation are suppressed. Large corporations buy the inventions, and then they bury them. I know that sounds pessimistic, but the main thing that you need to do is to be aware of this. If you become aware of this, then start a movement to reduce this in your area. That will be good.

There is some evidence that in prehistory there were technologies that were cleaner and more connected to the environment. Now, as you said, modern versions of these have been suppressed. Are these ancient advanced technologies just mythology or is there some truth that has filtered down and also been suppressed along with the technology?

The race of beings that existed in really ancient times was not completely third dimensional. They were much more telepathic than the current human race. You do not have the capabilities that they had at that time, although some of those capabilities are being revived now. Planetary issues of most importance in the near future involve water—the scarcity of water. Electronic smog is another issue. Those environmental issues are currently contributing factors to the high stress levels on the planet. If the stress levels are not dealt with by people meditating or reducing stress in other appropriate ways, war will result.

If we are to correct the imbalance between electronic equipment and human beings, do human beings evolve in the direction of becoming more compatible with electronic devices, or do machines evolve to become less invasive?

No, human beings should not have to evolve to become more compatible with electronic devices, although large corporations probably would like that. The most ideal thing at the present time, considering that sixty percent of the population is allergic to electro-magnetic frequencies, is to reduce the amount of contact through shielding and through less use of electromagnetic machinery and gadgetry. You must reduce the number of radio, television and mobile phone towers emitting these signals. Individuals need to protect themselves by various devices out in the market place even now. People need to assume they are sensitive until proven otherwise.

As the earth shifts into a higher vibratory dimension, people will become more sensitive rather than less sensitive to these energies. The percentages of people allergic to EMF's are going to increase over time. Whether they are genetically marked or not, with the earth raising its vibration, these EMF's will be even more out of sync with the vibratory shift. Sensitivity to these energies actually is an indication that the individual is already vibrating at a higher dimensional level.

Seraphim Blueprint energies will help you to ground and balance, so that you can better handle these inappropriate negative energies. Even with the assistance of the Seraphim energies, you will not be one hundred percent protected. Living sensitive beings are basically allergic to these electro-magnetic frequencies. While about sixty percent of the population is sensitive now, the percentages are going to rapidly increase. In ten years time eighty percent of the population will be sensitive. Rather than getting better, things are going to get worse, so more shielding and protection have to be used to protect human beings and other animals. At the moment, multinational corporations are not concerned with this issue, so you must spread the message through word of mouth that it is not good to use electric devices close to your body, such as electric blankets, hair dryers, or clock radios by the bed.

Do we need to unplug most electrical appliances from power points when not in use?

Yes. Most people do not know this, but when you use a remote control device, the equipment is actually on one hundred percent of the time.

Relation between Humans and Angels

In comparison to angels, are we as humans more vulnerable once we learn the Seraphim energies to negative energies or less vulnerable?

We have strength in numbers. Think of me as a lightening rod, taking the biggest hits from any negative energy. You are helping me by working with me and making my work useful and usable and putting it out there. No one has been doing this for a very long time.

I have had to shoulder too much of the burden of balancing earth energies. So you are helping, and I am able to shift some of the burden to your shoulders, but am still taking most of the major shocks of negativity. Ask Ruth if anyone who has taken these classes has complained about being psychically attacked. She will tell you that it has not been an issue so far. If it were to become an issue, I am sure that I can think of some remedy for that situation.

As one becomes more powerful (in an occupation, profession or any endeavor), one gets more responsibilities, and some can be warding off or averting the danger before it arises. Normally, the more powerful you are, the more powerful the adversary. So if you are not very powerful, you don't have to worry. In other words, Ruth has to worry more than you have to worry, and I have to worry all of the time.

Destiny of Planet Earth

There are channeled guides such as Kryon who talk about planet Earth as having a particular destiny, using the term "the only planet of free choice." The Seraphic Blueprint involves the galaxy, but not specifically this planet. I wonder how these two are related. Specifically, are there other beings with free choice in the galaxy?

There are other beings with free choice throughout the galaxy. Whenever you come to a local place, whether it is a town, a city, or a country, you want to make the natives feel happy. I think it's a bit of flattery that

Kryon and the other channels use. I do not agree with the opinion that Earth is that unique, although it's a very cosmopolitan place. It's considered to be one of the most beautiful places in the galaxy. It's like a resort for the galaxy.

Does it interfere with our spirituality or growth to allow us to be flattered?

Yes, I recommend that you ignore these statements and get to the heart of the matter. It's just an example of courtesy. It's what anybody does who is being polite and is a guest in someone else's home.

Fundamentalism versus Openness

There seems to be a change in the structure of communications on the planet. On the one hand, there is openness, and on the other there is a strong reaction to that, a falling back, or wanting to fall back to fundamentalism. How do you view the battle between the two? How can we make things easier?

Assuming that you don't just mean religious fundamentalism, but a more generalized literal reading of laws both religious and secular, then it would be a good idea to look at universal natural laws for a way to understand the processes involved more smoothly. The universal plan is one of creation, maintenance and destruction. We have to continually create new things, and they will be maintained for some time. Then even those things will be destroyed. A snowplough analogy might be useful here. In order to go forward, the snowplough must push the dirty snow aside. We still have to move forward, but we are aware that some of it gets impacted on the side and actually has to be carried away. People are in different stages of their own personal evolution. Some of them need lots of rules and regulations to function and feel safe, while others have achieved sufficient internal balance to feel safe in many varying external circumstances. Just an intellectual understanding of the idea that individuals have different homeostatic points of feeling good about the cultural norms they have chosen in their pre-birth plan will help you to feel a bit more comfortable on this planet.

When you speak of creation, maintenance and destruction, is war a natural part of that destruction?

Yes, it is. Every war is not equally necessary, but war is a natural phenomenon of this planet. There are, however, better ways of doing things. It's just that when people are not creative, when human beings fail in their creativity, then, sometimes, war is the only means of clearing the way. War is a major stress release, just like an earthquake or volcano.

> When human beings fail in their creativity, then, sometimes, war is the one means of clearing the way. War is a major stress release, just like an earthquake or volcano.

Is there anything we can do to ease that process?

Mainly, it's a question of working on yourselves and

being good examples for your friends, relatives, and neighbors. If we are participating in spiritual practices, we lead by example in our neighborhood, city, or town. Peace is based upon the individual being at peace within him or herself. It's very hard to change other people, but we can change ourselves. Prioritizing your life so that you put more attention on spiritual growth is always important, especially in times like these when there are all these threats. If you align yourself with the Seraphic energies, you are surfing on top of the wave.

Related to that last question on ancient cultures, there seems to be a lot of evidence, or at least hearsay, of them having destroyed themselves on various occasions. This seems related to the comments you made about stress. What are the chances that it will happen again to a large part of the population? What comments can you offer?

Nature will balance itself in one way or the other. The question is whether it will be smooth or not so smooth, and that's where we can make a difference. You see, the people in this room are those in the light, to be a little flattering. Those in the light need to lead. A large proportion of people don't know which way to go. They don't know whether to follow the dark or the light. We need to take the bull by the horns and lead. Reach out to other people who are not in your small group of friends and do not know this work and do not understand this work. Bring them in.

Are there any governments in power that are of the Light?

(Laughs) Mmm, let me see. I guess I have to say 'no.'

It has been said that a lot of dire predictions that had been made have in fact not come true, and won't— or at least the negativity of the predicted event has been lessened because of the spiritual work that we've been doing.

That's true. That's true.

What about the situation in America now?

That's a big question. What specifically are you concerned about?

Security issues.

You mean terrorists?

Yes.

Many people are jealous of America. I think jealousy is the basis of the attacks on America. Jealousy can garb itself in religious formats and sound holy. America advertised its "perfect" lifestyle on television and in the movies, thereby raising people's expectations for what can be achieved in their part of the world. So that is what's being reaped now.

How soon will a government of the Light appear on Earth and where?

Good question. Let's do the "how soon" part first. Within 37 years. That's good news actually. That means you will still all be here. (Laughs) I shouldn't say we will still all be here, but at least something will be happening here. Let's see. Where? It will take place in North Africa, where Algeria is presently.

Do you think we should rely on governments? Thirty-seven years is a long time to wait and it's not really worth waiting for.

Absolutely not! Do not rely on governments. Governments are a reflection of people's power and people's consciousness, not vice versa. Your governments do not lead you; you lead your governments because governments reflect the consciousness of the people.

Is it possible for human beings to achieve ascension?

The whole planet is ascending together. It's not like suddenly some of you are going to disappear into thin air. It's not like that. It's like you won't even notice, because your vibration is being raised with the planet as a whole. With everyone's vibration being raised, no one's going to disappear. It's just you are going into a higher vibrational state. It's not going to be a huge shift. In the old way of thinking, the year 2012 was very significant. It did signify an Armageddon type event. That has changed and has been postponed. If it were to occur, it is more likely to occur about 2040 not 2012. Hopefully, it will be postponed or will no longer be necessary by then. Again, there are different scenarios to how life on this planet can play out. It's in your hands.

There are things we are doing to the water and the air, though that's like a slow death, because once it's done, we won't be able to reverse the damage.

The planet has ways of healing itself, whether you are here or not here. I think the main question is whether you are here to see the healing take place. I don't think it's clear yet. The damage is significant but the storms that are occurring because of damage to the environment are going to become intense. They alone might wipe the slate clean or cause human beings to rethink everything. If there are droughts in some parts of the world that prevent people from eating who are used to eating, then things might change.

Is there something we can do to help world hunger that hasn't been done yet? Something creative?

Community gardening is very, very important. Wherever there is a space in a city like this, there should be a community garden. It will teach people how to get back to nature. It will give them some reason to protect nature. Community gardening is a very important lesson for this planet, even in urban areas. So teaching people how to grow their own food would be a good idea.

Does China have a future role in the world's spiritual development?

China has been called a sleeping giant. It is clear that China has been waking up, but when most people think of the sleeping giant metaphor they think in terms of China's economic and military development.

China is an awakening giant spiritually as well.

The so-called development community, including non-governmental organizations, has begun focusing more on emergency on the one hand and poverty elimination on the other hand. Where is the development community going in connection with spirituality?

It's very important that there be linkage; that there start to be linkage between spirituality and some of this kind of work. I don't know who is going to reach out first. But if the Circle of Light [Tokyo private group meeting since 1989] or somebody in this organization can start bringing these links together that would be very good. Linkage would be great. You know, you have a conference where you invite both groups to come together. The Circle of Light can be that umbrella organization bringing together appropriate groups.

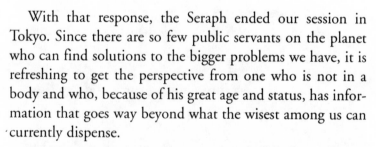

With that response, the Seraph ended our session in Tokyo. Since there are so few public servants on the planet who can find solutions to the bigger problems we have, it is refreshing to get the perspective from one who is not in a body and who, because of his great age and status, has information that goes way beyond what the wisest among us can currently dispense.

Yes, the Seraph has made himself available to you because these times of great change and global integration require our urgent cooperation in order to replenish our own energy and create an ongoing way to heal the planet. My sincerest hope in writing this book is to share with you the Seraph's incredible healing gifts and give you a few easy ways to continue to enjoy these beautiful energies while taking your next steps on the path.

Epilogue

When I think about all the recent interest in angels, I can see the natural progression within my own lifetime leading to this trend. "The generation of the sixties, in its search for peace and freedom from traditional authority, began to explore exotic cultures and religions, partly from curiosity and partly from a desire to know the ultimate reality." These young people were mainly North Americans and Europeans who had the finances and the leisure to travel to the ends of the earth. Breaking through cultural restrictions also led to their experimenting with hallucinogenic drugs, a practice that continues to wax and wane in many societies even now.

From the viewpoint of the angelic orders, the cultural transformation of the sixties provided the angels with a unique opportunity to contact those of us who were sensitive to exploring the further recesses of our minds directly. Since we were opening ourselves to subtle experiences of all kinds, it was as though we were knocking on the angels' doors asking, "Who lives here?" Angels had waited a long time for this opportunity. We were ready to communicate.

In forming any new relationship there is a getting-to-know-you period in which pleasantries and compliments are exchanged. In terms of angel and human interaction this took the form of small groups of people gathering around sensitive channelers to hear the wisdom of non-physical beings, such as extraterrestrials (E. T.'s), Spirit Guides and, in some cases, angels. The angels and E.T.'s tended to compliment the audiences attending such gatherings; and the novelty of the experiences, combined with this love-fest, enticed many people.

In the eighties and nineties a channeling craze blossomed. Many who attended these meetings felt the higher vibrations of the "visitors" to our earth plane and came away refreshed from the experience and amazed at the wisdom received. I remember my own excitement about attending a Bashar E. T. channeling and my fascination with the rapid-fire speech of the channeler. Such speech convinced me of the reality of the experience, for he seemed to be processing information much more quickly than a human brain can handle.

By the year 2000, however, the get-acquainted phase between non-physical beings and humans was wrapping up. The channelers were no longer drawing huge crowds. In fact the New Age movement experienced a quiet phase worldwide. It felt like its time might have passed. This was especially noticeable in the United States and Britain.

What people didn't realize is that after making new friends, occasionally the friendship evolves into a partnership. The angels were ready to partner with us, not as superior beings, but as equals. As Timothy Wyllie brilliantly wrote in his book *Dolphins, ET's and Angels*:

> The angels also maintain that we have a quality that they do not possess: the intuitive, creative spark-that wild leap into weirdness that can so often initiate whole new ways of perceiving reality.

Implicit within this constant sense of support [from the angels] is an important point that has thrown many others off course in the past and one that, incidentally, the angels themselves lay great stress on: we should not treat them as gods or infallible gurus, or in any way give away our power to them. Rather, our challenge is to accept who we truly are and to realize that the angels are ministering to the One who dwells within us every bit as much and more, most likely, than they are to us.

As in any proper partnership, the various partners bring different skills to the table. Angels have hundreds of thousands of years of experience associated with Earth and all the knowledge they thereby accumulated. Imagine the length of their résumés. They have a great sense of the sweep of history and the supreme interdependence of everything. They can thrill humanity and other species with energetic washes that both cleanse and heal. Being from another realm, however, they lack a sense of Earth time and frequently fail to show up when you need them most. Humans, if I were to generalize, are great organizers, both spatially in our third dimensional reality and temporally in our twenty-four-hour daily framework. Human beings can visualize a grand project and be responsible for carrying it out in great detail over long stretches of time.

Angels have hundreds of thousands of years of experience associated with Earth and all the knowledge they thereby accumulated. Imagine the length of their résumés.

Although I am oversimplifying the comparison between angels and humans, it must be emphasized that nothing is static in the universe. Every type of being is evolving. As humans are evolving in the direction of returning to God, angels are evolving toward becoming more grounded—and yes, more physical like us.

When I think of this tendency of angels, what comes to mind is the brilliant writing of Nora Ephron for the movie "Michael," which was a fictional account of Archangel Michael's earthly visitation to one small motel in Iowa. Michael, played by John Travolta, had some bad Earth habits like smoking and dowsing everything he ate with sugar. Ephron's brilliant portrayal of this great archangel enjoying the physicality of his temporary residence in a human body struck me as a real possibility and further confirmed for me that both humans and angels desire to have a full range of abilities and expression.

Although today there are many spiritual healing modalities available, these times may require even more help from the highest angelic sources. I am therefore honored to join Santoria, the inspiration for this book, in bringing you the astonishing information about these angelic energies and how they may be experienced and utilized by everyone.

Ruth Rendely

Healers I Respect

Andrew Johnston, an Australian energy healer, who practices what he calls "Resonance Healing." He uses homeopathic frequencies contained within a pendant worn on the body for a month at a time. He has developed these disks for imbalances including low energy, stress, blocked self-love, and other spiritual and emotional imbalances. He can work from hair samples. Contact him on **energyhealth@hotmail.com.**

Mother Meera, a self-proclaimed avatar, born in India in 1960 and residing in Schaumburg, Germany. People flock to her from all over the world to receive her darshan, her silent bestowal of grace and light through her gaze and touch. In her own words, she discusses her status:

"Avatars come from the Divine, while self-realized persons go to the Divine. Avatars are always one with God and never lose awareness of the Divine, unlike gurus who began ignorant. To become self-realized people—through spiritual practice, meditation, and japa—[gurus] work hard and then reap the fruit. Since they have worked strenuously, they expect others to work as they have; they do not have as much patience as do divine personalities. Also, Avatars can change things faster."

Reverend Joseph Martinez (1941—1995) A gifted Philippine Psychic Surgeon, a former Catholic monk who left the church, and instead taught a combination of Christian tenets, esoteric truths, and the Integral Yoga of Sri Aurobindo. His sense of humor, deep spiritual wisdom and practical approach to life made him truly loved by all who came into contact with him. I had the privilege of knowing him the last two months of his life.

Bruno Gröning (1906—1959) Known as an extraordinary miracle healer in Germany after World War II, he was hounded by the medical establishment and the clergy, partly because he was a simple laborer with no training in either medicine or theology. I consider him, however, to be an avatar that is now working from the other side, healing thousands of people every day. He is especially effective treating those with addictions.

Some Favorite Books

(That the Seraph also likes)

Autobiography of a Yogi by Paramahansa Yogananda, c.1946.

Maharishi Mahesh Yogi on the Bhagavad Gita—A New Translation and Commentary, c. 1967.

How To Know God: The Yoga Aphorisms of Patanjali. Translated by Swami Prabhavananda and Christopher Isherwood, c. 1953.

Manual of the Warrior of Light by Paulo Coelho, c. 1997

The Chalice and The Blade: Our History Our Future by Riane Eisler, c.1987.

The Great Turning: From Empire to Earth Community by David C. Korten, c.2006.

Linda Goodman's Star Signs, c. 1987.

Anything by **Nora Ephron.**

Glossary

Alice Bailey (1880—1949) An early leader of the Theosophical Society, she became famous for writing 24 books transmitted by a Tibetan spirit guide named Dwahl Kuhl. Her books created a body of esoteric teachings about ancient wisdom, religion, philosophy and contemporary events from 1919 to 1949, and are still popular today.

Angel A spiritual being discussed in many religions, including Buddhism and Hinduism. According to the three prominent monotheistic faiths, Christianity, Judaism and Islam, angels typically act as messengers of God.

Angel healing Some angels specialize in emitting energies that restore health, or wholeness, to other entities, such as human beings, animals, and plants. Such angels vary in their healing abilities. Some transfer energy once, or only when called upon, while others transfer energy that works continuously and silently with that other entity. Angels who are capable of communicating with humans can initiate individuals with latent healing abilities that are compatible with those of that particular angel. In such an initiation, angelic healing energies are "installed" in a person who can then retransmit them in full strength to anyone who also has such latent healing abilities.

Angelology A branch of theology that deals with a hierarchical system of angels, messengers, celestial powers or emanations, and the study of these systems. It primarily relates to Kabbalistic Judaism and to Christianity, where it is one of the ten major branches of theology.

Archangel A superior or higher-ranking angel. Archangels are found in a number of religious traditions, including Christianity, Islam, Judaism and Zoroastrianism.

Atlantis (Cf. Greek "the Island of Atlas") is the name of an island first mentioned and described by the classical Greek philosopher Plato. According to him this island, lying "beyond the pillars of Hercules," was a naval power that had conquered many parts of Western Europe and Africa. Soon after a failed invasion of Athens, Atlantis sank in the waves "in a single day and night of misfortune" due to a natural catastrophe which occurred 9,000 years before Plato's time. Some historians consider Atlantis to be an entirely mythical place.

Attunement An attunement is an initiation or a physical transmission of a specific energy.

Avatar (Cf. Sanskrit "descent"). An avatar is an incarnation, or manifestation of God on earth, taking a form in accordance to the requirements of the age in which the incarnation occurs.

Babaji A well-known avatar. Paramahansa Yogananda introduced him to the West in his best-selling *Autobiography of a Yogi* (1946), and later accounts have claimed him to be nearly 1,800 years old.

Chakra A Sanskrit word meaning "wheel" that has evolved from Hindu sources to mean radiating energy centers in the human body. These centers result from the mixing of spiritual energies that enter the body from the top of the head with earth energies that enter through the feet. At seven major designated centers in the trunk of the body and head, these two flows of energy meet and form whirlpools, much as water at a river's mouth meets the tide from the ocean and forms whirlpools. The chakras can run smoothly or there can be blockages, which eventually result in physical malfunctioning in that part of the body.

Channeling The transmission of information to or through a person (the channel or medium) from a spirit or other "supernatural" entity outside the mind (or self) of the channel.

Chi/ki A Chinese word meaning energy, specifically the vital energy of which all things are formed. Also known as prana, it is a fundamental concept of traditional Chinese healing. Ki (the Japanese term) is believed to be part of everything that exists, as in "life force" or "spiritual energy." It is most often translated as "energy flow," or literally as "air" or "breath."

Crystal healing Crystal healers claim that every living organism has a "vibrational energy system," which includes chakras, subtle bodies and meridians. By using the appropriate crystals one can "tune" an energy system, or balance energies, thus improving well-being.

Darshan Receipt of the special enlightening energies that emanate from a spiritual teacher. One receives this energy in an audience with, or by merely being in the presence of such a teacher. This can be a private audience, or may be attended by many thousands of people. Darshan can even emanate from the photograph of a highly enlightened being.

Dwahl Kuhl The Tibetan spirit guide mentioned in Alice

Bailey's books as her main informant and inspiration for her writings.

Ecumatschii The recently channeled Atlantean name of the Seraphim Blueprint system in Atlantean times.

Energy healing Energy Healing is a holistic approach to facilitating the healing of living organisms. Some energy healers remove internal blockages in the patient, and some use external sources of spiritual energy that might be available to them either from birth or from some training or initiation.

Feng Shui The ancient Chinese practice of the placement and arrangement of space, both within and outside of buildings. The term actually translates as Wind/Water, and when its rules are practiced faithfully, Feng Shui is purported to bring about harmony with the environment.

Gaia This Greek name for the mother earth goddess was adopted by the scientist James Lovelock in the 1960's to encapsulate his then revolutionary theory that the earth functions as a single, self-sustaining organism. His theory is now widely accepted, and has been used in New Age circles to reframe the way humanity views our home planet.

Grounding (or being Grounded) In esoteric terms, grounding is what is required to achieve full body/soul fusion. The concept derives from a term used with electrical equipment when that is actually connected physically to the ground, so that voltage is taken as zero—hence the name. Used in connection with the human body, it appears that living organisms operate with a great deal of bioelectrical energy that also requires "earthing," so as to not overcharge, or lose homeostatic balance.

Guardian angel A guardian angel is a spirit who is believed to protect and to guide a particular person. The concept of tutelary angels and their hierarchy was extensively developed in Christianity in the 5th century.

Holographic Initially Dennis Gabor (the father of holography) named the phenomenon in 1947 for an advanced form of photography that allowed images to be viewed three-dimensionally. The word hologram is derived from the Greek words "holos" meaning whole or complete and "gram" meaning message. In New Age circles, the term has come to mean that the complete whole exists in the smallest division of that whole.

Initiation The act of transferring of powers, especially of a spiritual nature from one person to another. In the context of ritual magic and esotericism, an initiation is considered to cause a fundamental process of change to begin within the person being initiated. The person conducting the initiation (the initiator), being in possession of a certain power or state of being, transfers this power or state to the person being initiated.

Kabbalah (Hebrew: קַבָּלָה) literally means a "receiving", in the sense of a "received tradition". Kabbalah is an esoteric form of Jewish mysticism that attempts to reveal hidden mystical insights in the Hebrew Bible and offers mystical insight into divine nature.

Karma The law of psycho-spiritual growth that involves an equal and opposite reaction for every action.

Karmic clearing Karmic clearing is a form of healing. These are techniques to "burn" the "seeds" of negative karma for someone before they produce their "fruit" (negative life events).

Ki (see chi)

Life-force energy (see chi)

Maharishi Mahesh Yogi Born Mahesh Prasad Varma, Maharishi is the creator of Transcendental Meditation (TM) and leader of the Transcendental Meditation Movement, based on the principles of meditation espoused by the Adi Shankara (c. 788-820 CE), and taught by his own master, Brahmananda Saraswati.

Opener A small empowered egg-shaped stone used by students of the Seraphim Blueprint.

Pendulum A divining tool, usually a small weighted object, of either wood, or stone, attached to a chain, used by psychics and water diviners since ancient times.

Prana A Sanskrit word meaning 'breath' and refers to a vital, life-sustaining force of living beings and vital energy in natural processes of the universe. Prana is a central concept in Eastern medicine and Yoga where it is believed to flow through a network of fine subtle channels called nadi. The three main channels are: the ida, the pingala, and the sushumna. See also Chi and Ki.

Pre-birth Council A little known belief in New Age circles according to which a group of spiritual high beings advise a soul before birth for the purpose of preparing that soul for its life-lessons in the coming incarnation.

Psychic A person with a paranormal ability such as clairvoyance, clairaudience, premonition and precognition.

Sacred geometry The archetypal geometric patterns of nature can be used for healing and for meditation. Sacred geometry is used in all cultures to build churches, temples, mosques, and other sacred places. The belief associated with sacred geometry is that the mathematical ratios implicit in geometry also inform cosmologies, music, and various other art forms. They are observable, too, in the structure of plants, animals, crystals, star systems, and so on throughout the micro—and macrocosm. One reason archetypal geometric patterns are said to be sacred is related to a certain stage of spiritual practice, in which these patterns appear within the primal form of the visual field of the practitioner when his or her eyes are closed in meditation. The first stage of this appears as a milky light, which fills the visual field and constitutes its primal form. In some tantric traditions, this white light is identified as soma (see following). At the next stage of development, this light then resolves itself into geometrical configurations that can be found in mandalas, yantras, and the patterns of rose windows in gothic churches.

Sephirot In the Kabbalah of Judaism, there are ten attributes that God created and through which he can project himself to the universe and man. These emanations manifest not only in the physical part of the universe, but also in the metaphysical one.

Seraph A single angel of the Seraphim Order. The plural form is "Seraphim." This is the group of angels mentioned as being closest to the throne of God in the Old Testament of Judaism. These angels are regarded as important to the three desert religions of Judaism, Christianity and Islam.

Seraphim See "Seraph."

Solar Angel Helena Blavatsky, cofounder of the Theosophical Society, introduced the term "Solar Angel" to the West from Tibetan sources. She posited that these angels came to Earth 18 million years ago in response to an appeal from our Planetary Logos, the sentient being known as Gaia. According to Blavatsky, Gaia became concerned with humanity's slow mental evolutionary progress and introduced these angels to help us along.

Soma According to the Indo-Aryan tradition, soma is a plant with hallucinogenic properties used in rituals. The plant was called soma by the Indians and haoma by the Iranians. Although some of the descendants of these peoples still perform their rituals, the identity of this sacred plant has been lost. In the Vedic tradition, soma is also considered to be a milky-white substance, that some believe the body synthesized as a by-product when the individual becomes enlightened. Soma is also the root of the English word "psychosomatic."

Theosophical Society Theosophy, literally "knowledge of the divine," was revived in the nineteenth century by Helena Petrovna Blavatsky to designate her religious philosophy which holds that all religions are attempts by humanity to approach the absolute, and that each religion therefore has a portion of the truth. Together with Henry Steel Olcott, William Quan Judge, and others, Blavatsky founded the Theosophical Society in 1875.

Thrones (Also known as Ophanim in Hebrew) A classification of angels under many Christian angelic hierarchies. They are the carriers of the throne of God, hence the name.

Transcendental Meditation A sitting, eyes-closed meditation that uses a seed word or mantra to encourage the practitioner to relax, release stress and ultimately become enlightened.

Tree-of-Life A mystical concept within the Kabbalah of Judaism which is used to understand the nature of God and the manner in which He created the world out of nothing. The Kabbalists developed this concept into a full model of reality, using the tree to depict a "map" of Creation. The tree of life has been called the "cosmology" of the Kabbalah.

Trisagion A Greek code word attributed to the Seraphim, which means "thrice holy," and stands for the Biblical phrase, "Holy, Holy, Holy is the Lord of Hosts."

Walk-in An ancient concept first described in Hinduism whose modern name originated in the Spiritualist faith and was popularized by the related, but not identical New Age movements and beliefs. A walk-in is thought to be a person whose original soul has departed his or her body and has been replaced with a new soul.

Worldwide Courses, Trainings & Consultations

The Seraphim Blueprint Levels are taken in sequence, starting with Seraphim Healing. These initiations are facilitated in one or two-day workshops, either by a teacher who is personally present, or long distance via conference calls or through the Internet. Even if you live in a remote rural area, you will be able to receive these energies worldwide if you have access to these forms of communication.

Currently, Ruth and some fifty teachers give these workshops. As of this printing, there are active teachers in America, Japan, Australia and Malaysia. To locate a teacher near you, please consult the Seraphim Blueprint website, as it will contain the most up-to-date information: **www.seraphimblueprint.com**, or Ruth's website: **www.ruthstar.com**. If you wish to receive information by regular mail, enclose a self-addressed stamped envelope and mail to: Seraphim Blueprint, P.O. Box 1224, Fairfield, Iowa 52556, U.S.A, or to Seraphim Blueprint, P.O. Box 50, The Blue Mountains, NSW 2783, Australia.

Teacher Training

The Seraph and Ruth wish to make qualified teachers around the world to meet the growing demand for this work. If you are interested in becoming a teacher, the current requirements include completion of the first three levels of the Blueprint, and submission of an application to Ruth at **ruthestar@gmail.com.**

Consultations & Teleconferencing

Ruth continues to give private readings and consultations, as her schedule allows. To receive a free quarterly Seraphim Blueprint Newsletter online or participate in teleconferences in which the Seraph will share his energies live, please send your details and e-mail address to **ruthestar@gmail.com.** You can also call her on her direct line from North America at 1(800) 736-3351.

Website **www.SeraphimBlueprint.com**

About the Author

R uth has led two lives. The more traditional one has been as a university history lecturer and occasional writer for the Washington Post and the Mainichi Graphic. A graduate of George Washington University, she was a grantee at the East-West Center at the University of Hawaii where she received her master's degree in East Asian history. She subsequently completed doctoral studies in American intellectual history at the University of Iowa. Her recent life has been as a meditation instructor, healer, and spiritual teacher. She resides in the Blue Mountains near Sydney, Australia.

Printed in the United States
70969LV00001B/145-348